Contents

Removing Wallpaper?

(READ THIS FIRST)

A Mini Course in Wall Restoration

B.C. George

ISBN (Print): 978-1-7355269-0-4

ISBN (Digital): 978-1-7355269-1-1

Chapter One –

Overview

Contained in these pages are descriptions of the techniques and tools that are necessary for **top notch perfection** when you want to turn a papered wall into a painted one. You do not need to have any experience to follow the steps and get an amazing result. This stuff is not rocket science, and reading this book, even if you don't read super-fast, will be worth the time invested.

The intended audience is wide ranging. First, this mini-course will greatly help those who have recently purchased a home and want to redecorate. Having a road map of best practices in front of you while completing the steps does wonders for interpersonal communication when working as a team. Secondly, as a journeyman decorator who's done this hundreds of times, I want to share what I've learned with the apprentices. Mastering this skill will make them more valuable to an employer.

For best results in the wall restoration project, you want to have a sense of where the process is heading at every stage in the game. I implore you to read this course through completely before actually starting the work. Then use the Table of Contents to hone in on each part of the process as you complete the project.

WHAT IS HERE

We'll talk about removing residential wallcovering first. Generally, peoples' first encounter with this process occurs in a house, usually in some state of being rehabbed. Many well-intentioned DIY beginnings get abandoned or hired out ($$$) because a few critical steps were missed. The omitted steps cause a downstream ripple effect that leaves the finished product less than perfect and the only memories of "re-doing the kitchen" are painful ones. This course will fix that by empowering you with the knowledge and techniques for a successful renovation project.

Next, we'll consider commercial wallcovering. It's a different animal because it's thicker, wider, and generally comes off the wall in one layer. It also loves to bring part of the wall along with it. We'll talk about how to best peel it off, and then how to deal with any damage that inevitably occurs in the process.

There is even a section for those situations where removal has shown itself to be impossible – usually when the wall becomes so damaged from peeling that the drywall falls apart internally. You will be shown how to go over top of wallpaper without the final product looking like, well, painted-up wallpaper.

As these processes are presented there will be discussions of common myths and misconceptions. Any advice presented here that runs contrary to conventional wisdom is backed up by a simple description of how to see for yourself.

Myth No. 1 – Host a Painting Party – "with 5 of us we'll be done real fast…"

My advice is **don't do it.** This is a process that goes on for days and uses messy materials and sharp objects. Your buddies will show up, get in the way and drink all the beer - leaving you with even more mess to clean and several steps remaining to be completed. There is **drying time** involved and you can only go so far in the course of a day before something needs to dry completely. Save the party for the big reveal.

When planning the sequence of smaller tasks that combine for the finished project, you will be given options that suit a range of budgets – when that's appropriate. Certain steps **require** spending enough money to buy the right product, and other steps can be accomplished with more common materials. Whenever specific products are mentioned, please be aware that no manufacturers have partnered with the author and their products are mentioned on merit alone. They may not be available in your area, so I will try to describe them in general terms as well as by the name brand.

WHAT IS NOT HERE

In this book you will not find an exhaustive list of all the tools you need to have in front of you before the project begins. That seems overwhelming and unnecessary, not to mention expensive. Tools will be introduced as the process for which they are used is being described. I will describe a range of options of tool selection where that's appropriate, and if part of the process requires a quality, specific tool, that will be pointed out.

Also, very little ink is devoted to preparing the work area. The reason is because this may or may not matter. A house being flipped will typically get new flooring *after* the ceilings and walls have been painted. A house or office with carpeting that stays will need better prep work. Use common sense for this. When a particular process is very messy it will be mentioned. What to do about it is up to you and your particular situation. This book is more about the process and how to get a first-class final look.

Finally, you won't find glossy pictures or links to DIY videos here. Every situation is unique. Each material is unique, and was installed by humans at a particular point in time, over top of who-knows-how-many layers of previous wallcovering. A stylized and polished video version of everything going perfectly is not going to help - what you need to know is right here, in the contents of the paperback book or the digital version. Any diagrams are presented with apologies using crude stick figures doing the work and arrows showing the direction of force. So, let's dig in!

Chapter 2

Stripping Residential Wallcoverings

The anatomy of typical residential goods is helpful to understand before attempting removal. Most products are two layers thick – a paper base layer and a shinier, water resistant top layer that can be paper, vinyl, or a wide range of other durable films. Rarely have I encountered a residential wallcovering that comes off both layers at once. The process described in this book will assume that is not possible in your case either, and we will be removing the two layers separately.

Myth No.2 – you gotta steam the wallpaper off

Well, actually, no you don't. The steamer technique will not be covered here. I think there's a filmstrip from the 1970's that covers this outdated, very messy, and overly destructive technique. Not interested? Read on.

TOP LAYER

You'll need some specific tools for this part. Beginning with a scraper; on the high end, you can purchase a wallpaper scraper that is made specifically for stripping this top layer. It has a sturdy handle and replaceable blades that are very sharp. They are effective, but I haven't used one in years for two reasons: the blades are expensive and they tend to make more gouges in the wall. What I prefer is a simple 4" drywall joint knife that I've dedicated to be a permanent scraper. They quickly become very sharp, cost around five bucks and last quite a while.

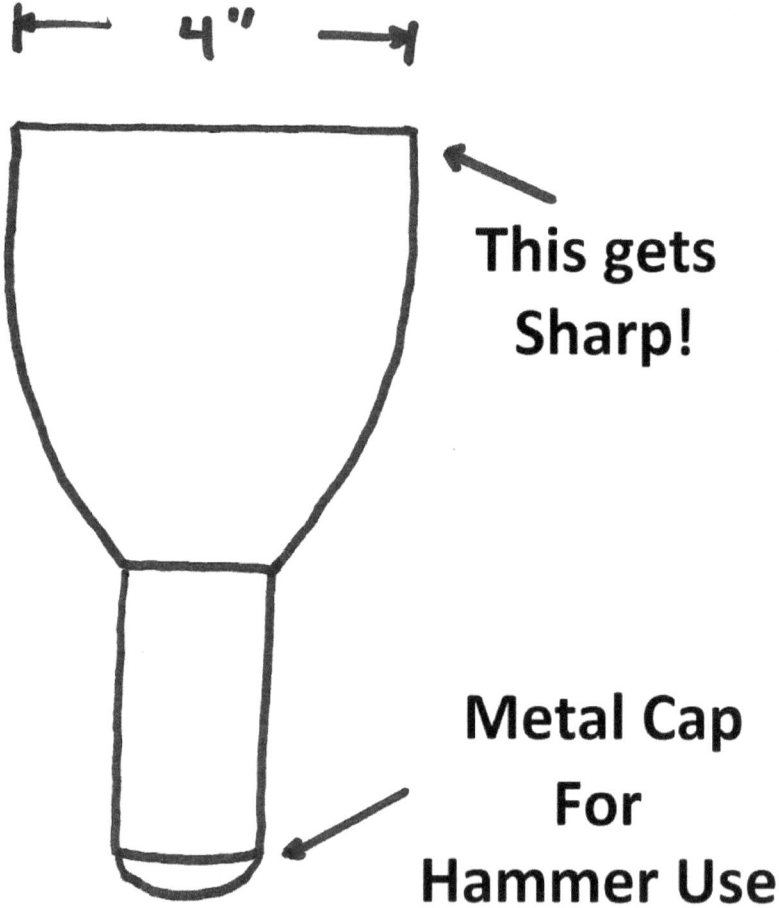

This gets Sharp!

Metal Cap For Hammer Use

Myth No. 3 – You need to pre-soak the top layer with removal solution

Save this stuff for the next layer. Even with a perforating device (*Paper Tiger*) the solution won't penetrate most common top layers.

Before starting removal of the top layer, take off the cover plates from light switches and power outlets. *Replace the screws* and set the plates aside. Make sure picture hangers are gone and there are no nails, tacks or screws left on the wall.

Techniques for removing the top layer will vary somewhat according to the specific texture and thickness of material, but generally you will need to use a slicing motion to get some loose material started, then peel what you can until it finds a weak spot and rips. Repeat as necessary.

By now you have a pile of paper-ish material on the floor. I hope they are big pieces, but if not, don't feel like you did anything wrong. Sometimes the top layer comes off in sheets and sometimes you're left with nothing but little scraps.

BOTTOM LAYER

What's left on the wall is referred to as the backing. It's usually made of paper and this is the part that interacts with the paste during installation. I've never been able to completely remove this layer without water in 30 years of experience. Beware - this step is **messy**. If you need to save the flooring, now is the time to put down plastic and tape the edge to the top of the baseboards using blue painter's tape. I prefer 1.5" wide. Plastic used on floors should be at least 1 mil thick to withstand your feet during this process.

That being said, you will need to use a *removal solution* to soak the backing fully, then your trusty 4" scraping knife to do the dirty work. You have a range of budget options here; on the low end try just hot water as the removal solution. 80% of the time it works just fine. If you need some more bite, add some vinegar if you can stand the smell. The absolute best removal solutions will contain an active enzyme that breaks down wallpaper paste. Dilute this stuff with water. In the Midwestern U.S. a common leader is the product *DIF* by the *Zinsser* Company.

> *Myth No. 4 – You need a garden sprayer to apply the removal solution*
>
> This is ridiculous and hugely messy. You can apply the solution cleaner and deeper with a bucket and sponge, or set up a paint roller and use a tray or bucket. Be careful to apply pressure during the up-stroke of the roller, not the down-stroke, to avoid big pools on the floor.

Soak an area of such a size that you can scrape clean before it dries out and re-sticks. This will vary according to temperature, humidity, and local air movement. Use a paintbrush to soak narrow spots like door headers and the strip of wall between a corner and the trim of a door.

Brush dotted areas

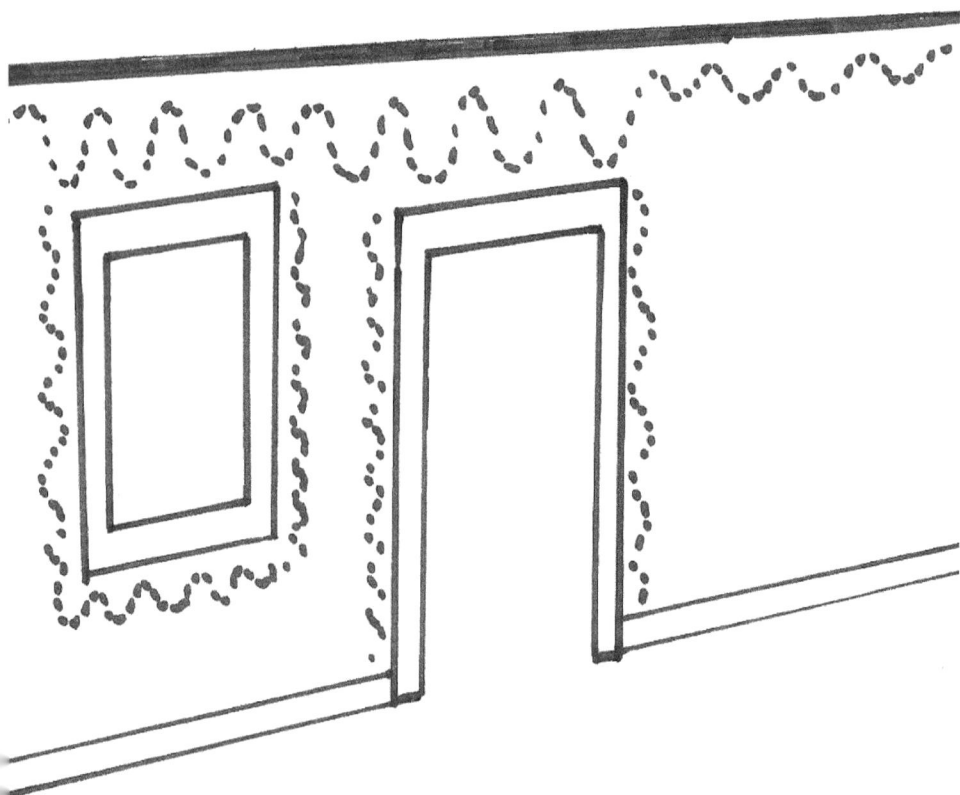

When this messy task is completed there will remain a hazy film of wallpaper paste on the wall. You have a choice to make – either wash the remaining paste off the wall or seal it up with a special sealing product. Painting or skim-coating directly over what remains is unacceptable. The moisture in paint or mud will re-activate the wallpaper paste, pulling and sliding along in ugly piles.

TO WASH OR TO SEAL

The more economical method is to wash the paste using the same removal solution you just used. Using a bucket and sponge, wet the paste thoroughly. Then use the 4" scraping knife to get the bulk of it off. A final pass with the sponge will get the crumbs.

Alternatively, you can apply a sealer to lock down any remaining paste. After the sealer is dried, the application of drywall mud *will not* reactivate the paste and your project can proceed without the disaster that would have occurred had this step been ignored!

Products used for the sealing step can vary. On the low end of the budget range, an exterior paint or primer may get the job done. An acrylic primer / sealer is even better (*Kilz by Zinsser* or *Seal Grip by PPG),* but there are products better made specifically for this task. In the Midwestern U.S. we use *Gardz* by *Zinsser* or *RX-35* by *Roman.*

I prefer the penetrating power of *Gardz.* It is runny and does not behave like paint. After curing overnight the wall becomes almost like plastic and is ready for the next step.

Roman's *RX-35* behaves more like latex paint, and although it does not penetrate like Gardz, it does work, and best of all it doesn't stink any worse than paint. Whichever sealer you choose, be sure to follow manufacturer's instructions for proper ventilation of the work area.

Back to washing paste... Even if you have successfully washed the remaining paste off the wall, there will undoubtedly be spots where the scraper damaged the drywall or the act of peeling one of the layers resulted in damage. If the brown paper of the drywall is showing, you need to lock this down by applying one of the above-mentioned sealers before repairing those spots.

If you are so lucky as to have removed wallpaper and washed the paste off without any damage to the walls, you may be able to proceed directly to priming and painting the dried surface. More likely, if what remains is looking rough, and you want a first class finished product, turn to Chapters 8 and 9.to learn the mud work.

If you chose instead to apply sealer (Chapter 6) and lock down any remaining paste, allow this to fully dry overnight before resuming work according to Chapters 8 and 9.

Chapter 3

Stripping Commercial Wallcoverings

This type of wallcovering is found in waiting rooms, medical suites, corner offices and public spaces. It is built and tested to withstand a certain measurable amount of abuse and fire resistance.

Like its narrower cousin, commercial "paper" is built in two layers. The backing interacts with the paste and is usually not made of paper. It is a sheet of either woven strands of polyester yarn or spun polypropylene strands. Upon this backing a layer of flexible vinyl is applied in a heated liquid state by a series of really impressive machines. When it cools, the two-layer vinyl is subjected to texture rollers and printing processes for an infinite variety of designs.

The ease at which commercial wallcovering is removed depends a great deal on how it was installed. The type of paste, whether the surface was sealed, painted, or bare drywall, and of course the material itself all play into how exactly it can be removed. Sometimes wallcovering that's installed on an exterior wall is ready to jump off the wall, but then there will be pieces elsewhere that refuse.

PRE – CUTTING

Begin by removing cover plates to light switches and electrical outlets. Also remove picture hangers, nails and screws where possible. You will need an appropriate **cutting tool** and **safety**

gear for the next step. On the budget end, a snap-blade mini-utility knife will suffice. If you can spend a little more, consider purchasing a refillable snap blade knife like a 9mm *Olfa*. In either case, your fingers will thank you if you also purchase a pair of **cut resistant gloves**. These have rubber coated fingers for grip, and are available all around the world.

There is probably a drop-ceiling in the room you are working on. The wallcovering may or may not be installed behind the corner molding of the drop ceiling. Run your knife along the bottom edge of the ceiling to be sure. The amount of pressure you need to slice completely through the wallcovering will vary according to thickness of the material. Try to adjust your technique so that the vinyl is fully cut but the wall stays relatively unscarred.

Also slice along the top of the baseboard or rubber cove base. Even if the base is getting removed this step is worth it in the long run. Run the tip of your razor knife *below* the top edge of the vinyl base. Cut around any permanent wall devices like fire alarms, data ports and card readers. During construction, it is common for electrical outlets to be installed after the wallcovering is complete. To avoid damaging the outlet during removal, you must cut around the little rings that are part of the receptacle body.

Trim Here

If there was a bulletin board or something else on the wall that employed some type of wall anchor (plastic plugs, "molly bolts", etc.) you should make a cut around these anchors as well. This will help avoid ripping and allow you to remove the wallcovering in big sheets.

STRIPPING THE VINYL

The good news is that unlike residential goods, this stuff comes off all at once. The bad news is it likes to bring parts of the wall along with it. Again, so much is dependent on how the "paper" was installed, but following this technique will afford you the best chance to eliminate blisters and bubbles in the final painted product.

There will be dry paste, room dust, drywall dust and fibers of paper flying through the air for everyone to breathe during the stripping process. Take the appropriate precautions to protect the contents of the room and especially your lungs. On the high end, I recommend a NIOSH approved half face respirator with HEPA cartridges. On the cheap end, a bandana or an ear loop face mask will suffice.

Start from the top – find a seam or start from an easy corner, and pull **directly downward in parallel to the wall's face**. This is SO important!

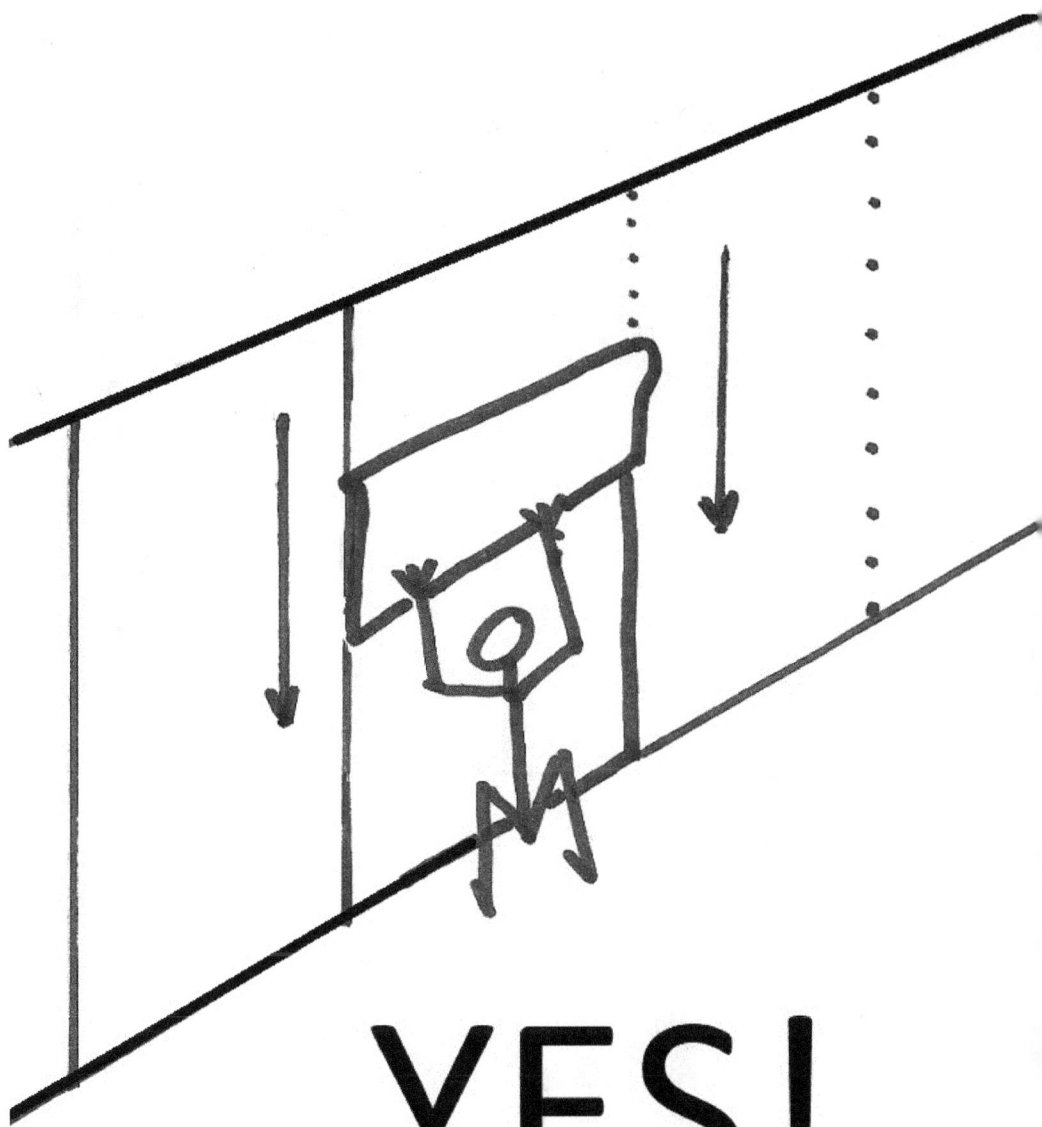

YES!

DO NOT pull backward on the vinyl as this will encourage the various layers that make up drywall to delaminate.

NO!

Lay the pieces on a clear spot of floor, one on top of the other with no wrinkles. Save one of the better pieces to use as two free disposable drop cloths. When you've got 8 pieces or so on the pile, roll it up, tape it shut, and start a new one. This will leave you with a manageable size roll instead of something that breaks your back.

Make another pass through the area to check for loose ends. Do a thorough job of slicing and trimming all the little pieces away from windows, ledges, door trim, and all the other on-wall obstacles. When you're satisfied with the removal, it's time for an often overlooked step in the commercial wallcovering removal proces

Chapter 4

The Wall Whisperer

You've probably noticed that peeling away the commercial vinyl "paper" left your wall in a variety of states. Whether you're now looking at bare drywall, a formerly painted wall, damaged plaster or something else, there will be loose portions of some component of these walls, and they must be excised.

Myth #5 – You gotta cut "footballs" in the wall

One of the old ways of dealing with the loose spots was to use a razor knife to cut pointed ellipses around the damaged area. You're about to learn a better way.

DRYWALL WALLS – FORMERLY UNPAINTED

First, turn the music down. You need to be able to *hear* this part of the process. Go ahead and swirl your hands on the wall. As you run your hand in a sweeping motion, the sound created at the surface will vary according to how tightly bound the layers of paper that compose the drywall face remain.

Where everything is nice and tight, you will hear a deeper sound, like the whole panel of drywall vibrating and the general noise of a hand sliding on a wall. Where there are trouble spots, you will hear a hollow, higher pitched sound indicating voids in the layers of paper below. These are either created during the stripping process or existed before, and although using proper technique (pulling straight down, not outwards) can help avoid these hollow spots, they are bound to occur after stripping either commercial or residential wallcovering.

Use your sharpened 4" drywall knife to scrape away the hollow spots as you hear them. Continue each spot until the loose material is no more. Let the wall be the guide, and don't be afraid to peel away big chunks of drywall paper if it seems like *everything* is loose. In extreme cases, you may be left with no surface paper of the drywall at all, just brown paper and drywall mud at the seams, screws and corners.

Don't panic - you are saving yourself many steps in the future by performing this blister eradicating task. It's much better to handle this at the outset as opposed to later when there's mud, primer and paint on top of the blisters that start *right here*. It's not uncommon for me to fill a kitchen trash bag with nothing but these little scraps after stripping a small waiting room. After no more hollow spots are evident, you are ready for the section of this book on sealing the walls.

DRYWALL WALLS – FORMERLY PAINTED

These situations are especially frustrating. You have all the complications of "normal" removal mentioned above, plus the scattering of cured paint that will either stick to the wallpaper or stay behind on the wall – lurking with a hidden agenda. Visually inspect the remaining paint for signs of blisters. These must be painstakingly scraped away with your dedicated 4" scraping knife. Do not wet the walls; water won't help here. Run out each bad spot with your scraper until there is no more loose material. Now it's ready to seal. Skip ahead to **Sealing the Wall**.

PLASTER WALLS

The good news is plaster walls don't lend themselves to the blister effect that a drywall system can yield after stripping wallcovering. The bad news is that you're probably not dealing with just one layer of paper. In any case, remove all wallcoverings in the same, parallel-to-the-wall motion as described above.

Chances are there will be some loose plaster spots after removing the "paper." These need to be scraped out, and any dust that remains in holes should be swept out with an old paint brush or, better yet, vacuumed clean.

Although plaster walls won't have the same delamination problems like the drywall discussed above, you still need to seal up the wallcovering paste so that the application of patching compound and skimming mud will not reactivate it. The walls are ready for sealing.

Chapter 5

Overcoating

"This wallpaper simply WILL NOT come off the wall." Period.

Occasionally, this is really a thing. Once in a great while there comes a time when forced removal is too compromising to the wall system to be worth continuing. It happens in both residential and commercial settings, and it's impossible to predict the conditions that result in absolutely requiring an over-coat of drywall mud and then painting.

The steps below will show you how to make the old paper disappear under a freshly painted, crisp and new-looking wall. The trick is to get rid of all the signs that paper was once here by trimming away critical parts and then applying an over-coat of drywall mud to get rid of any texture left behind by the wallpaper.

The process for dealing with overcoating is basically the same for residential and commercial wallcoverings. First, examine all the seams for loose spots. Use your 4" dedicated scraping knife as a probe. Residential paper often overlaps at the seams. Be sure to remove all the overlap:

View on Edge

Seam Overlap

    Next, cut out the paper from the inside corners. Using a razor knife and cut resistant gloves, score a line 3" away from each inside corner and peel the material. It should be loose enough to remove a narrow strip like this:

Scored Edge

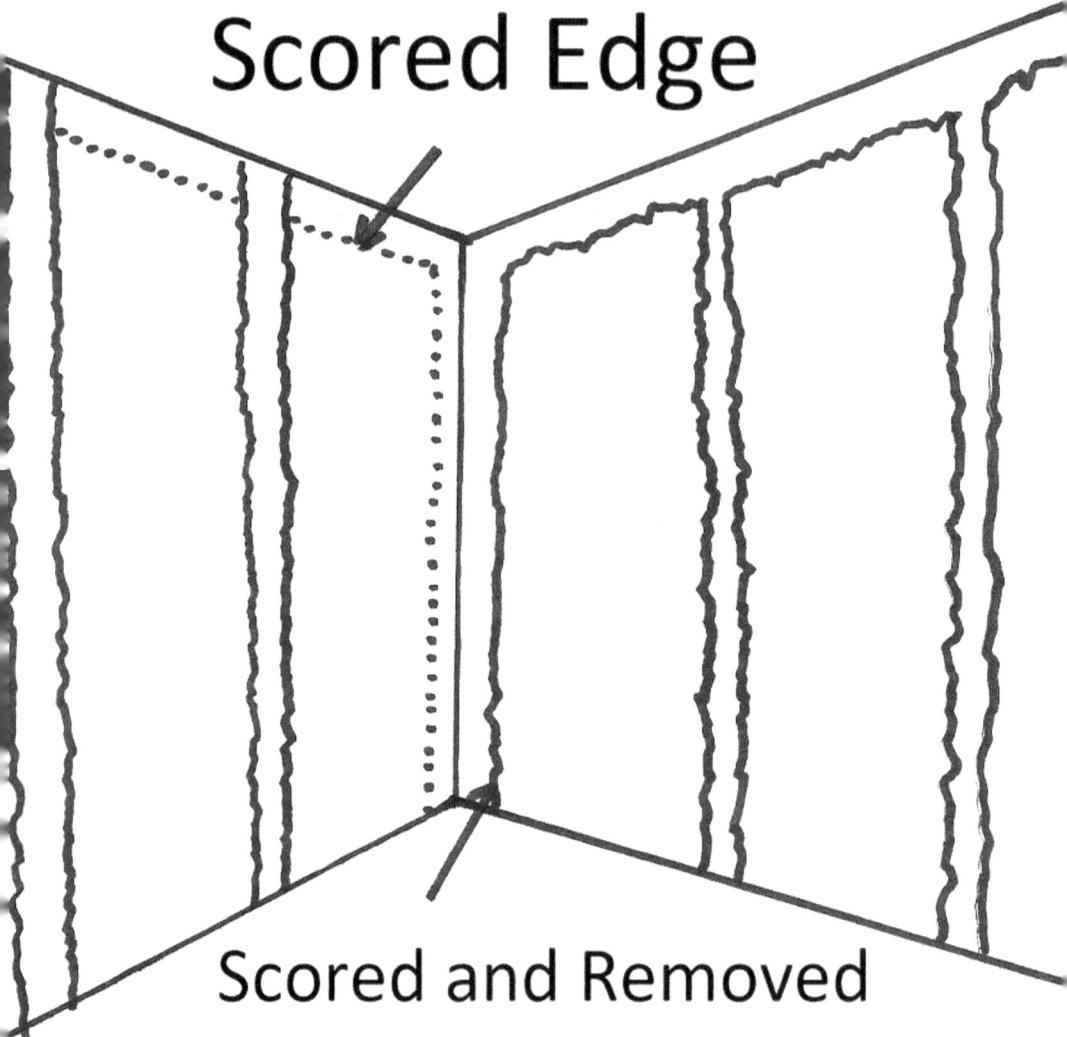

Scored and Removed

Next, cut a strip away from each outside corner by first running a knife along the very edge of the corner, the "bead" to fillet a very fine strip of material away:

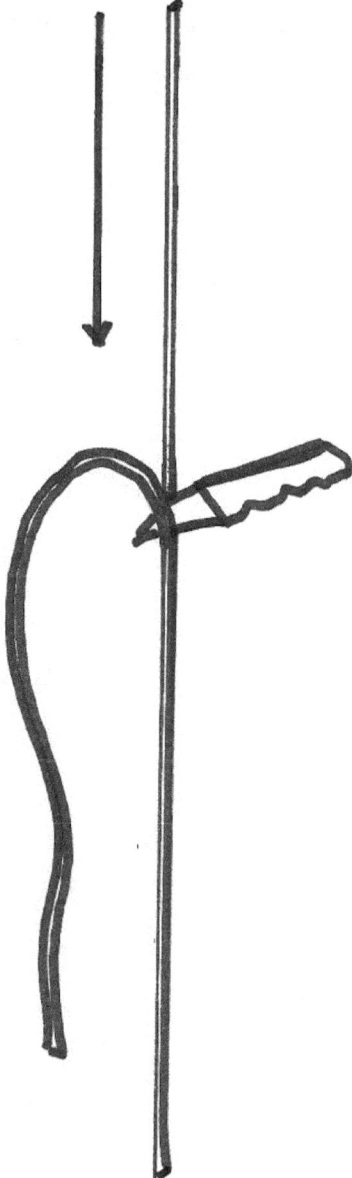

Then, score and peel the wallcovering about 4" back from the corner, on each side, from floor to ceiling. The first cut (the fillet) provided a relief so you can remove these two pieces and do little damage. Later on, when you spread a couple layers of mud to fill this void it looks as though the wallpaper was never there, and the corner's edge is nice and crisp.

All Corners and Seams Prepped

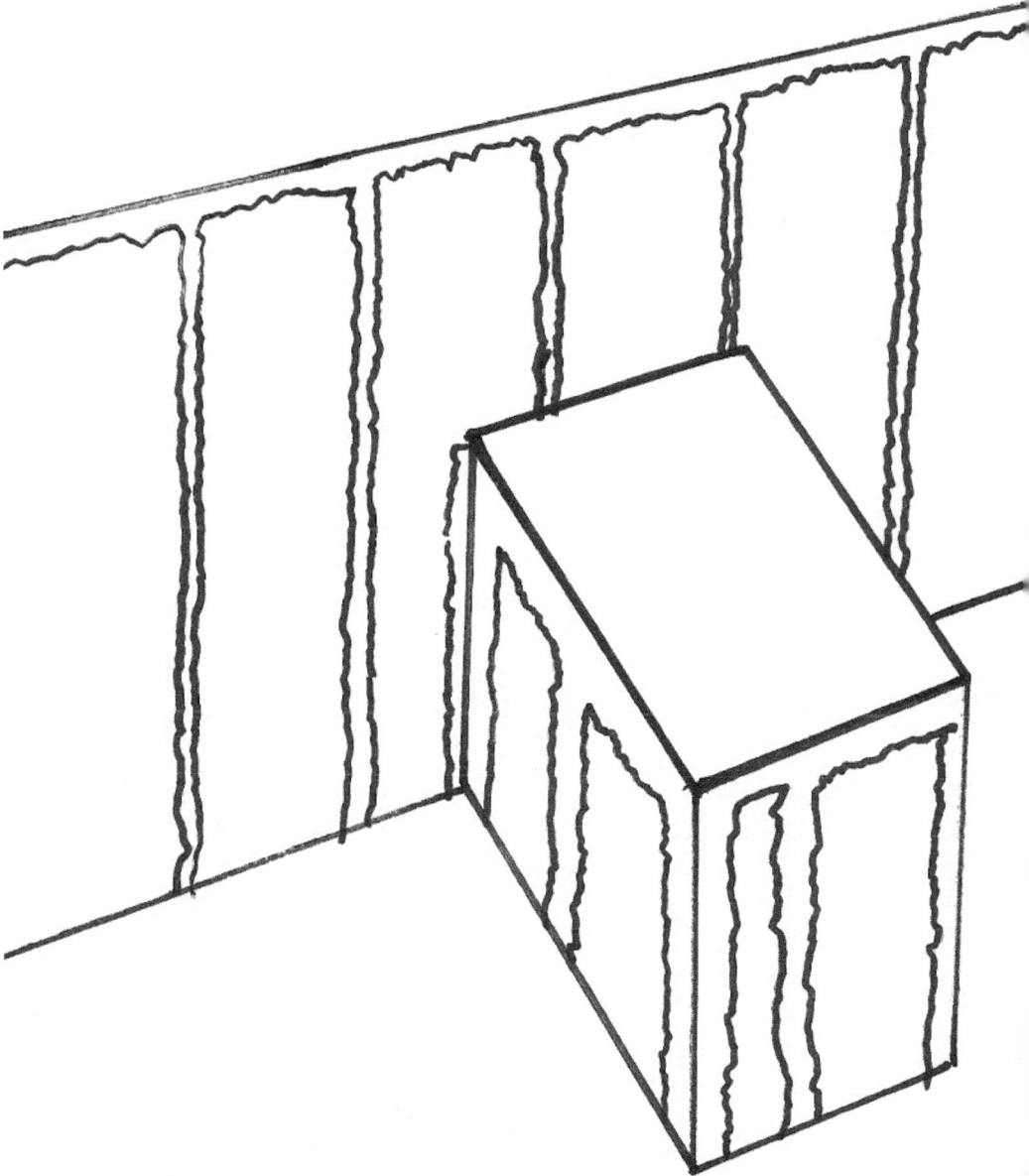

When all the corners are fully prepped and everything loose has been scraped away, the walls are ready for sealing. You will use a bonding primer in this case.

Chapter 6

Sealing the Walls

Applying a quality sealer will do two things; help damaged drywall become a better starting point for future layers, and lock down any remaining paste from the wallcovering that was just removed. Skipping this step will result in many more blisters from the damaged drywall, and a smearing effect when drywall mud is applied later.

CHOOSING A SEALER

All projects have a budget – and this is one area that can throw the initial budget way off. It is worth spending the money for a good sealer. Don't just use cheap primer. Any specific brands mentioned are from experience only, in the Midwestern U.S.A. None have partnered with the author or publisher for inclusion.

The *tools* required for the sealing process can be of a lesser quality than those that will be used for the final coats of finish paint. You can get the $2.00 roller sleeve and the throwaway brush for this step. **When we get to painting the finished product, you will need a quality brush and a quality roller sleeve**. They cost more than the "entire painting kit for $9.99." at the big box store. Prepare to spend about $15.00 for a decent wall brush and $7.00 just for the roller cover (½" nap) that goes on a 9" roller frame. An extension pole that adjusts is better than a broomstick, but either one may serve your needs.

** In the rare case that you will be skimming over wallcovering that could not be removed, I recommend a **bonding primer** to help the future layers of mud stick to a sometimes shiny surface that has been hand-printed and juice spilled for probably several years. Around here we mostly use PPG's *Seal Grip*, Sherwin Williams' *Extreme Bond Primer*, or *XIM* by Zinsser for this step. **

Now the thing to consider is the smell. Some of the old school sealers like *BIN* by Zinsser and pigmented shellac (lots of places make this) may be sufficient if odor is not an issue and the budget is tight. As mentioned before, my personal all-time favorite sealer for damaged drywall, *GARDZ* by Zinsser, has a strong ammonia smell for a couple hours and it's not the cheapest in the store. What I do like is how it penetrates the drywall and after curing overnight the walls feel almost like plastic.

If odor is an issue, there are still some very good remedies for sealing damaged drywall, locking down old wallcovering paste, and not gassing anyone out of the building. In my experience the best low-odor sealer is Roman's *Rx-35*. It doesn't penetrate like GARDZ, but a liberal application over a properly prepared wall gives great results. On the budget end of things, I've tried water-based *Kilz* by Zinsser and had mixed results. This is one of those areas where it doesn't pay to skimp, so I generally choose between *GARDZ* and *RX-35* depending on odor requirements.

Once you've chosen a sealer, give your walls one more look, checking for hollow spots and missed pieces of wallpaper. To avoid getting debris in the skimming mud during the next steps, run a broad drywall knife, a drywall sanding sponge or a sanding pole with 120 grit (or so) sandpaper across all wall surfaces.

You'll need a paint tray for the roller and a small work pot for your brush. Check that your work area is sufficiently covered up for a drippy, sometimes "splattery" procedure. Apply it similar to paint, but allow it to soak into damaged portions of drywall by reapplying immediately until the wall seems well saturated. Some of the sealing products are formulated to penetrate deep into the damaged drywall and lock up the matrix by curing into a near plastic-like state.

A tip for applying a runny sealer: Apply pressure to the roller on the upstroke, pushing a bead of sealer toward the ceiling, allowing it to soak on the way up.

APPLY

Applying pressure on the downstroke with a runny sealer will result in an absolute mess:

DO NOT APPLY

Use a brush to "cut in" the areas of the wall where the roller can't reach, just like painting. When everything is coated, allow the area proper drying time before proceeding to the next step. For best results, wait overnight.

There are warnings on the cans of sealer about ventilating the area. Please read these and take the instructions seriously. The use of a flammable sealer adds another layer of hazard – and these days the oil-based products are more expensive anyway, so try to stick with a water or acrylic based product.

Chapter 7

Mud Work – Tools and Products

DRYWALL TOOLS – HAND TOOLS

Time to invest in some drywall tools. Don't worry, you won't have to walk on stilts to get a first class look. You also don't have to buy the highest-end option to get that same look. When it comes to choosing knives, just look for ones that are straight. Hold them up to the light, and pick out a few broad knives like a 10" and an 8". The mid-width knives (6" to 3") are generally half-moon shaped, but again look for a straight edge and clean corners. Get as many different sizes as your budget will allow, 6" down to 3". You'll even need a small knife for the margins between a door and an adjacent wall. Think 1.5" or 1".

A cheap plastic mud pan with a metal blade actually works okay. Until you forget to wash and dry the metal strip. For best results, spend the extra $10 bill and get a stainless steel mud pan. Get something to sand with – anything from a simple abrasive sponge for $2 to a professional sanding pole will be fine. Lastly for the hand tools, get a cleaning brush to protect your tools after use. I use a simple dishwashing brush from the grocery store, but fancy brushes made just for drywall pans are available at supply houses or the big box stores.

DRYWALL MUD SELECTION

You will be using pre-mixed drywall compound for the bulk of this process. Look for the products called "lightweight all-purpose" joint compound. They will work the best for what you are doing, and they are the easiest to sand at the end. Confusingly, avoid products that simply say "all-purpose joint compound" but do not say "lightweight." This means the product is loaded down with glue, and is meant to be used primarily for taping new drywall joints. It's very hard to sand after drying and it's not what you need for this process. Specific brands of mud that I often use for this process: USG *Plus-3 Lightweight All-Purpose Joint Compound* (dark blue lid), LaFarge *Lite Blue Joint Compound*, and National Gypsum's *Lightweight Joint Compound*. If these brands are not available where you are, look for a pre-mixed drywall joint compound commonly used for intermediate (coating) applications.

Expect to use a five gallon bucket to coat the walls of an average bedroom. In order to make the pre-mixed mud usable, some amount of water must be blended into the pre-mix. The amount of water added will vary according to which step in the process you are performing. There are two ways to do this. The cheap way – which takes longer, and the other way where you acquire an electric drill with ½" chuck and a mud mixing paddle. Since you will be likely to use several buckets of mud on your project, consider the time of stirring water into each pan of drywall mud, hoping to keep it consistent from batch to batch, versus spinning up a whole bucket of drywall mud and then just scooping as needed.

IMPORTANT – always plug a mud mixing drill into a GFCI protected circuit! It can save your life!!

Chapter 8

Mud Work – Heavy Patching

At this point, the wallcovering is removed, all the loose drywall paper and/or loose plaster has been peeled and scraped away, and a generous application of sealer has been allowed to fully cure. If this doesn't sound accurate, go back and complete these crucial steps. Everything in this process builds upon the last step. You will have a first-class product if you take the time to ensure each step is completed.

Inspect the drywall and plaster for signs of fracture and cracking. Common spots are just above the corners of doors and windows. Apply **self-sticking fiberglass drywall joint tape** to fractures and cracks. *Very fine* cracks in plaster can be ignored as the two layers of skimming mud will cover them up. Consider caulking the inside corners before getting started with the mud.

Attack the deepest, most damaged portions first. Stir the joint compound, either with a drill and paddle or in the mud pan with a small knife, and add very little water for this first round of patches. Fill the low spots, smear over any cracks you have taped with fiberglass, and if removing wallpaper has left ridges between brown drywall paper and pre-existing mud work like corners and seams, now is the time to start levelling those transitions out.

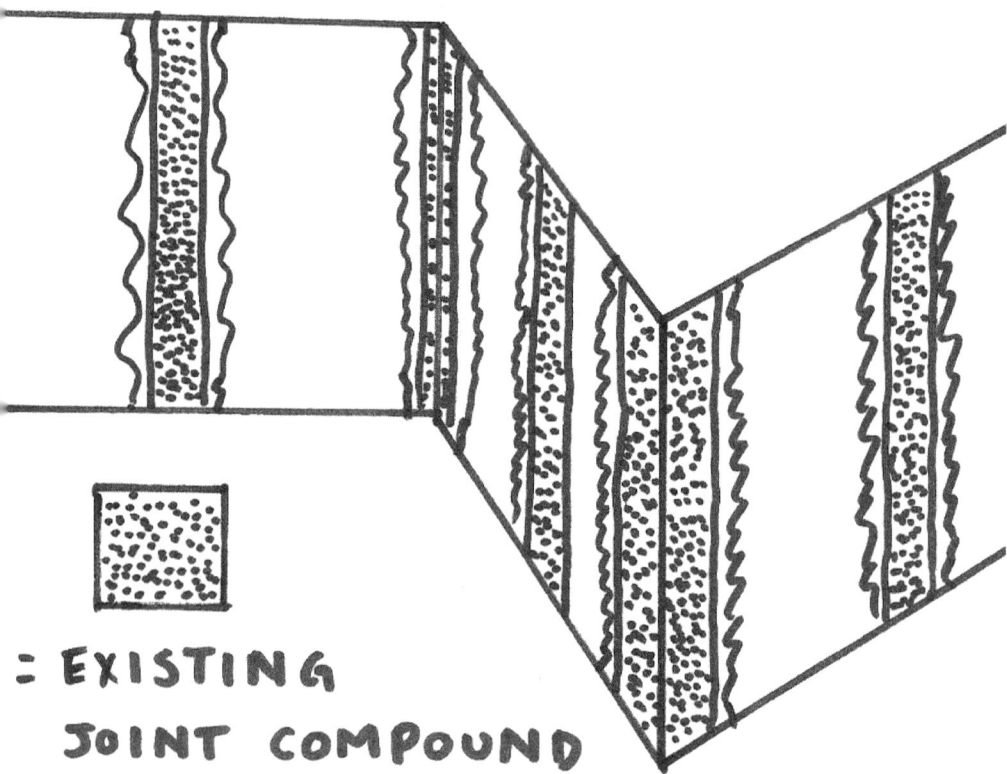

: EXISTING
JOINT COMPOUND

: FILL HERE

Apply a generous amount of compound to the area to be levelled. Just pile it up using an 8" broad knife. Don't try to smear and spread. Think of this as wall sculpture – simply apply way too much, then peel it back with the knife until you are left with a profile that makes the wall look flatter that it did before. It doesn't have to be pretty just yet – the more time you spend on the same area, the more you dig out the precious filling that creates the foundation for a flat look. Don't worry about leaving ridges, but do try to avoid dragging solids through the mud. Gouges take extra steps to fi, but a ridge can be scraped away in seconds during the next step.

Fill holes left by removing old picture hangers, and now is the time to decide if any unused electrical outlets are going to be patched over. The paint store sells really neat self-sticking mesh patches that actually work. There are dozens of other ways to patch an outlet (just ask the internet) but the point being NOW is the time to make those repairs. Check along the bottom of outside corners for evidence of impact damage. Dig out any loose drywall and fill with mud. When all the heavy patching is complete, allow your work to dry overnight. Some shrinkage is to be expected, but there are still two more layers to go and everything will turn out just fine.

"HOT MUD" – ADVANCED OPTION

If time is critical, or you want to try some advanced drywall techniques, there is the so-called "durabond" option. This word is the former trade name of the first example of a **setting-type** drywall joint compound. This is the stuff that comes in bags. It's never pre-mixed, because once water is added, a chemical reaction starts and in a number of minutes (that's usually printed on the bag) the liquid mud will become set almost like a soft version of concrete.

The benefit to using a setting-type compound for the heavy patching step is that once the stuff has set up you can go directly to the next step in the wall skimming process. The heavy patches will not be dry, but will be firm and able to support more layers of mud. There is also less shrinkage over the deepest of the repairs when using this option.

On the downside, the material is very alkaline, it causes skin irritation, and the dust is not safe to breathe. You also have a limited time in which to dispense with the material you prepared. A bag of USG's *20 Minute Lightweight Setting Type Joint Compound* has a working time of 20 minutes. If there is still mud in the pan at 22 minutes, it will be set up and un-spreadable. Must be thrown out, and all tools cleaned of this harsh material.

> *Myth #6 – Quick set mud will "dry" in the time printed on the bag*
>
> Not true. It takes nearly as long for the quick muds to *actually dry* as it does for the pre-mixed compounds. If you paint over wet mud, the paint will not stick. Don't do this. The only reason for using the hot muds on your project is to go over deep spots on the same day with drywall mud, not paint.

SKIM COATING PHASE 1.1 – HEAVY PATCHING OVER WALLCOVERING

In the rare case the wallcovering proved impossible to remove, you should have trimmed the corners and removed any loose paper at the seams by now. A sealer has been applied and allowed to cure. Now, mix up some joint compound to the consistency of peanut butter, and fill the spaces left by removing the strips of wallcovering that you forced off. This will typically be on both faces on an outside corner and both sides of an inside corner.

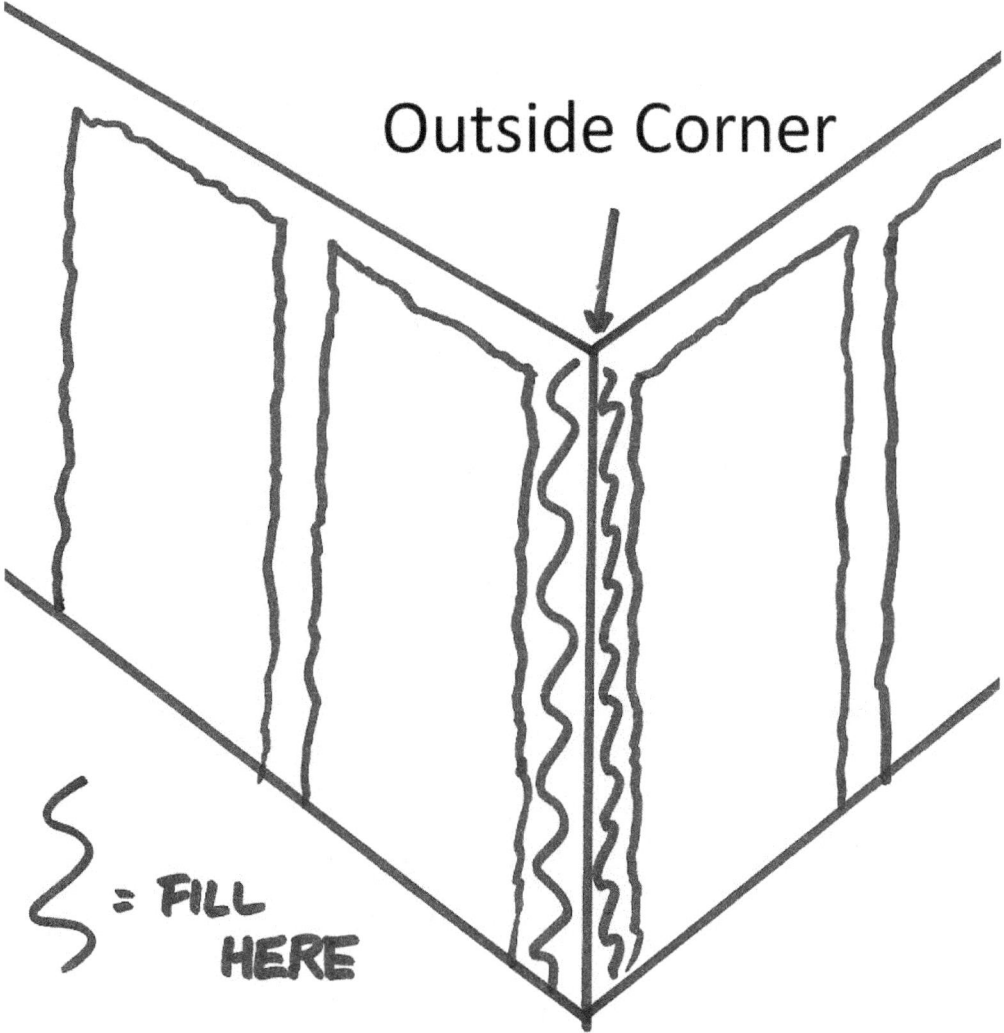

Outside Corner

$\lbrace$ = FILL HERE

I recommend filling inside corners using a side-swipe approach. Load plenty of material into the corner with an 8" broad knife, then start sculpting it back in a sideways motion until it looks like the mud and the existing wallpaper are in the same plane. It doesn't have to be pretty just yet, there's still another layer (maybe 2) to go. If you're feeling brave, you can try to coat both sides of the interior corners at once using this side-swipe approach. If time is of no concern, you can allow one side to dry before filling in the adjacent corner. Fill any other areas where loose paper was removed.

INSIDE CORNER

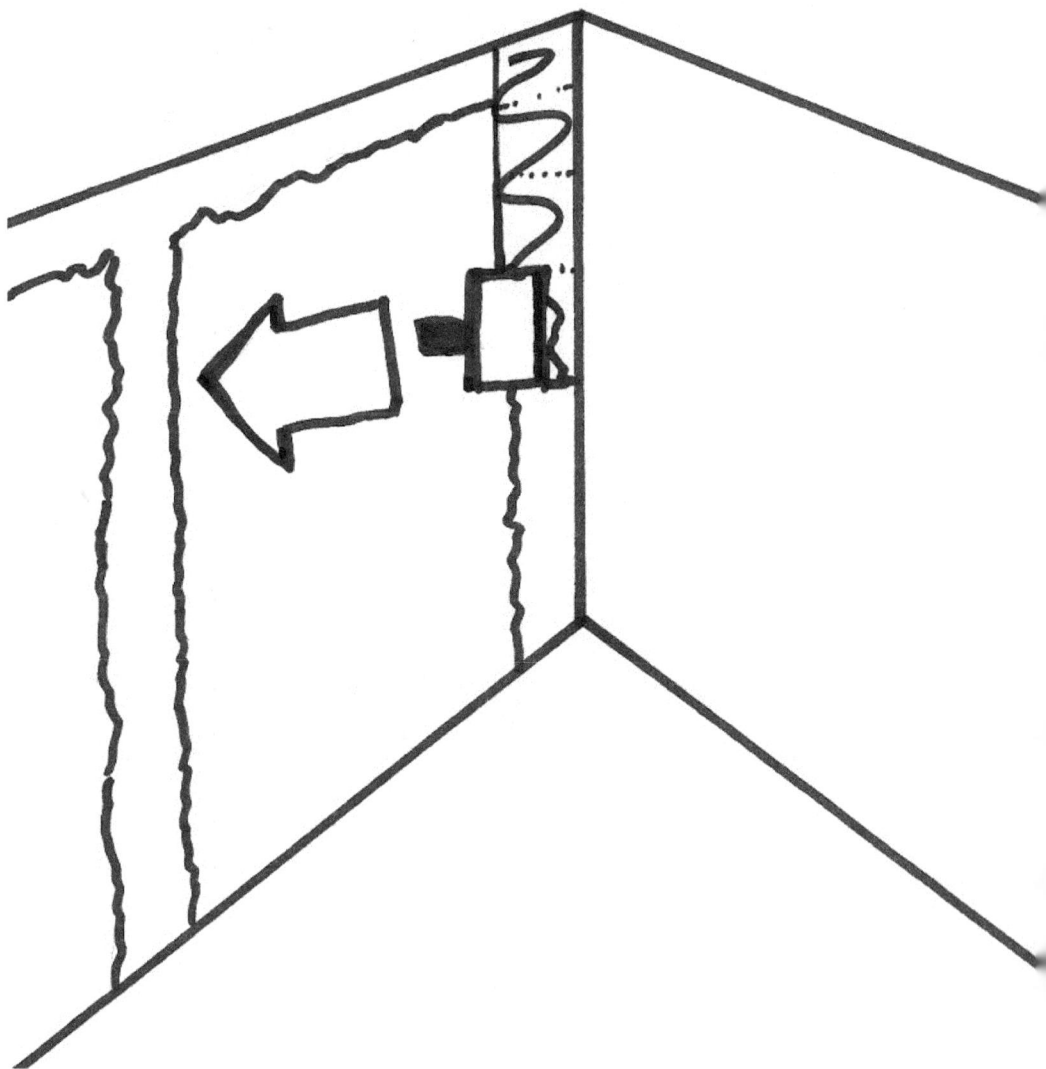

Allow this foundation layer to fully dry before proceeding to the next step,

Chapter 9

Mud Work – First Skim Coat

Now that all the deep spots have been filled and the cracks are repaired, it's time to give these old walls a new skin. At this point you'll need to decide on which method – knife or roller – you'll use to apply the skim coat. Decide now because you'll mix the mud with slightly more water to apply it with a roller, and slightly less to use the pan-and-knife method. The size of the work area is a big factor when making this decision. Are there large areas of open wall where a roller would be useful, or is everything "chopped up" by doors and windows? Personally, I am faster using the roller method. On the other hand, I know other experienced Journeymen like Dan Hammer who get great results but swear they are faster using the pan and knife approach.

PAN AND KNIFE APPLICATION

Using your 4" drywall knife, pull a few scoops of lightweight all-purpose joint compound from the bucket and into your mud pan. Stir it around some, then add enough water to make it the consistency of peanut butter. It should spread on the wall without causing fatigue. Apply the entire pan to a section of wall in an over-generous application. Then, using an 8' or 10' broad knife, peel away excess mud until what remains is a thick skin around 2/10 of an inch deep. Scrape the rejected joint compound back into the mud pan. Flatten what remains with a final pass of the knife, laying it down all the way and not picking up any more material. Repeat the process on another chunk of wall, paying special attention to the interface between the current and the previous section of wall. You don't want to run over mud that's been allowed to start drying.

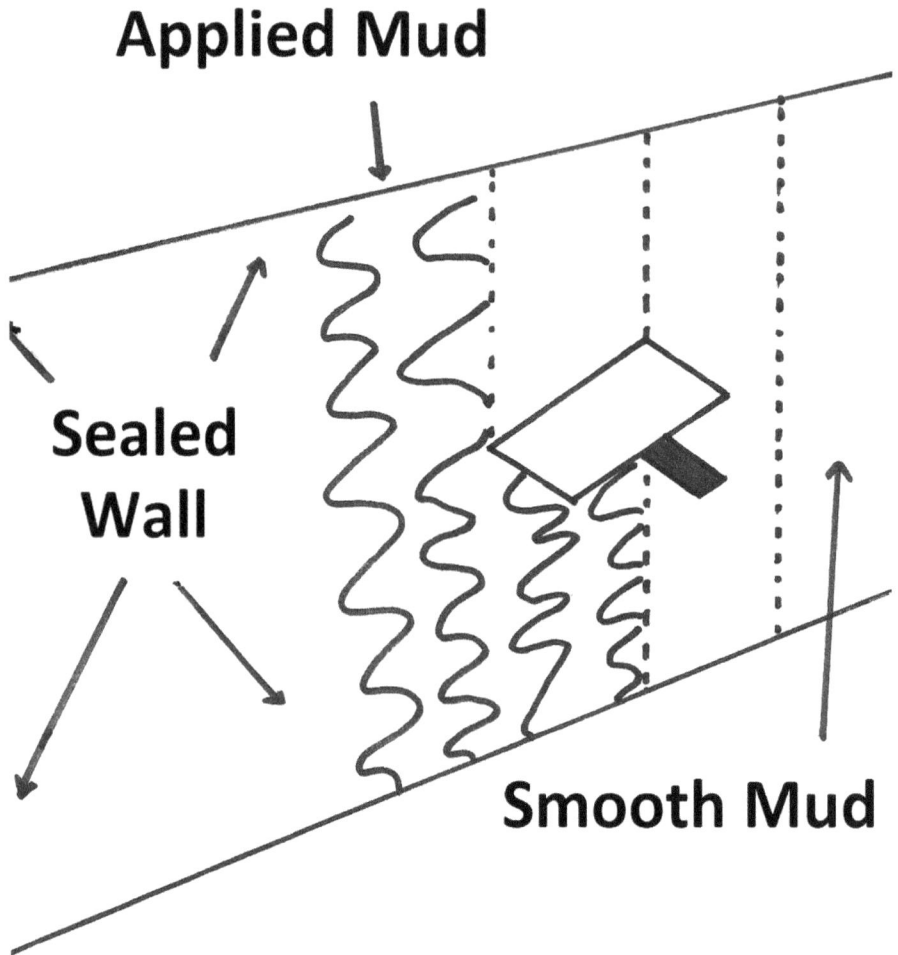

Applied Mud

Sealed Wall

Smooth Mud

It's tempting to use existing features like wood trim or a window frame to be a guide for your knife. Most of the time you end up with little ridges called chatter marks that are a pain to sand out. I recommend working from the largest areas to the smallest, working with the broad knives first, then the skinny ones. When approaching an inside corner, pull the finishing swipes sideways. This way you can do a complete corner, wet-to-wet, with decent results.

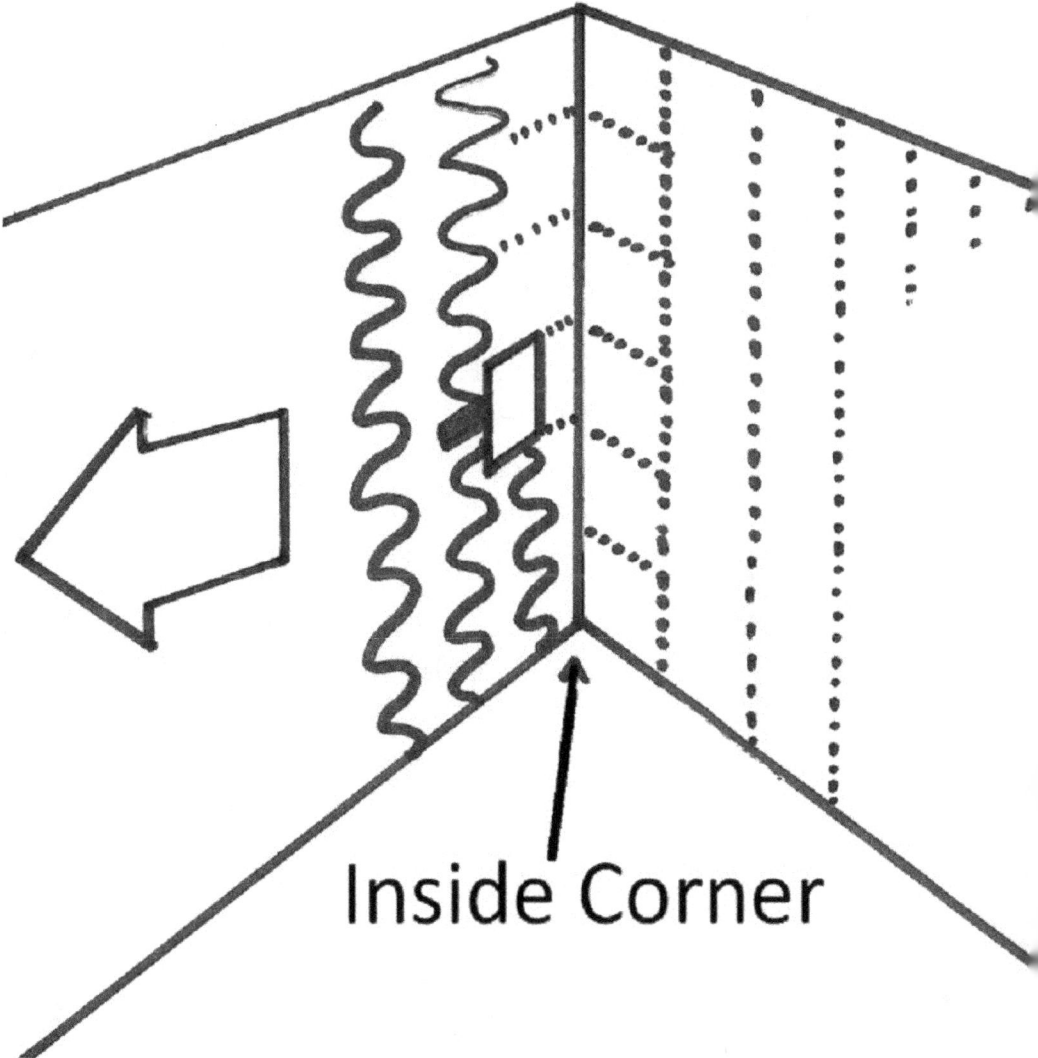

Inside Corner

Don't skip the little pieces of wall between the door and the adjacent wall. These "door margins" reveal more than you'd expect after the paint goes on. *Cover every square inch of wall with nearly 2/10 inch of drywall mud.*

One of the hardest things to learn is when to leave well enough alone. It's okay to leave lines and overlap marks when you work with mud. Gouges are bad, and hollow or voided spots will show in the end, so be sure to check for and erase any deep grooves or craters. As long as the wall has a new skin covering everything, the project is headed toward success.

At this point, the whole area needs to dry completely before moving on.

> *Myth #7 – get as much heat in the area as you can so it dries faster*

> In reality, it's *air movement* that does the drying. Adding heat sources that burn fossil fuels like kerosene or natural gas actually pump water into the room as a product of combustion. Get the air moving with fans, and be patient as the inside corners take the longest to dry.

When the mud is crisp and dry, the walls are ready for the section "Skim Coating Phase 3 – The Second Layer"

ROLLER APPLICATION

If the work area is of sufficient size and obstacle-free, a paint roller may be used to directly apply joint compound to the walls. You'll need to add enough water to the lightweight all-purpose joint compound so that the mud has the consistency of ketchup. Use a mud mixing paddle, not a paint paddle, attached to a sturdy drill with ½" chuck. Chop the mud with the paddle to get things loosened up, then add about a cup of water to get started. Run the drill clockwise to mix the water through the entire bucket. You will need to add more than the initial cup to get things the consistency of ketchup. Unfortunately I cannot provide an exact formula for the "perfect" skimming mud. Shelf time, seasonal variations in formula and those across manufacturers all contribute to an uncertain amount of water already in the mud. It will take some trial and error to get it right.

Check the work area to make sure things are covered up that need to be covered. Consider using a piece of masking tape over all power outlets. This process can be messy at first, but the technique described here can help minimize the mess.

A roller pole *is a must* for applying mud this way. Consider an adjustable roller pole with a quick connect device attaching the roller handle to the pole. This will save you time in tight spaces. Use a 9" paint roller with a ½" nap roller sleeve. Thicker roller sleeves won't hold any more mud than a ½" or even a 3/8" nap; in fact they just make applying the mud *evenly* all that more of a challenge. A dry roller is at first reluctant to pick up skimming mud, so give the top of the mud a smack to get some mud started onto the sleeve. Pull the roller toward you to force it rotating a bit. Smack again. Work that little bit of mud onto a small patch of wall, and the sleeve will be ready to pick up more mud on the next "smack."

Once the roller sleeve has been broken in and is picking up mud, resist the temptation to dunk the whole thing under the surface to load it. Try using a raking motion to load just the skin of the roller, and then knock the "tail" of mud away on the bucket's rim as you take the roller to the wall. With practice you can skim the walls of a carpeted office without really needing a drop cloth. For now, a piece of the old wallpaper makes a great disposable drop.

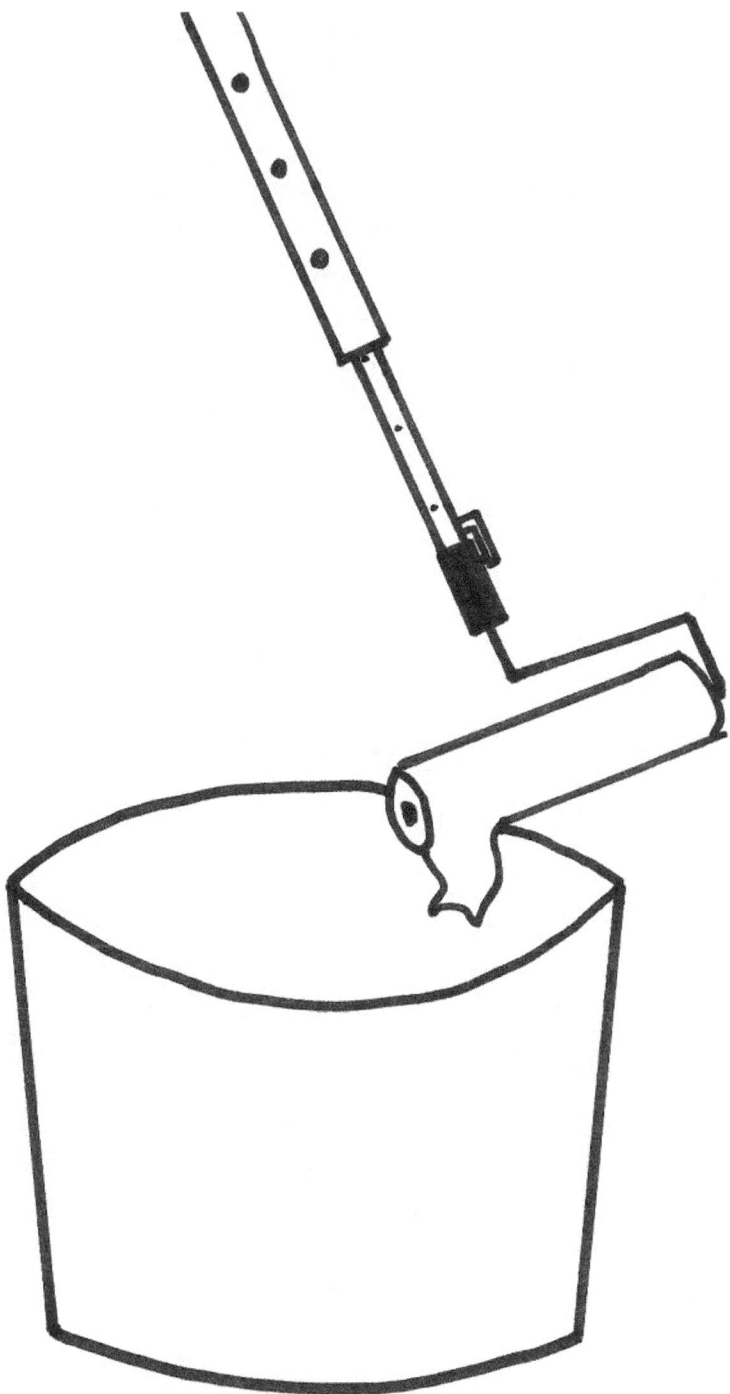

Bring it to the wall without hesitation, even adding a little "thump" as the roller makes contact. This helps the mud stay on the wall and off the floor.

Use your roller like a round trowel to smear mud in an even patch, as wide as the roller and about 3 feet in length. Don't worry about sliding the roller (it should slide), and don't try to stretch a dip of mud any further than *three feet long by nine inches (one roller) wide.* Repeat the dipping and smearing process about nine times, running each patch into the next. Set roller down and prepare to flatten the rolled area before it has a chance to start drying. (A bucket lid is a great wet roller holder).

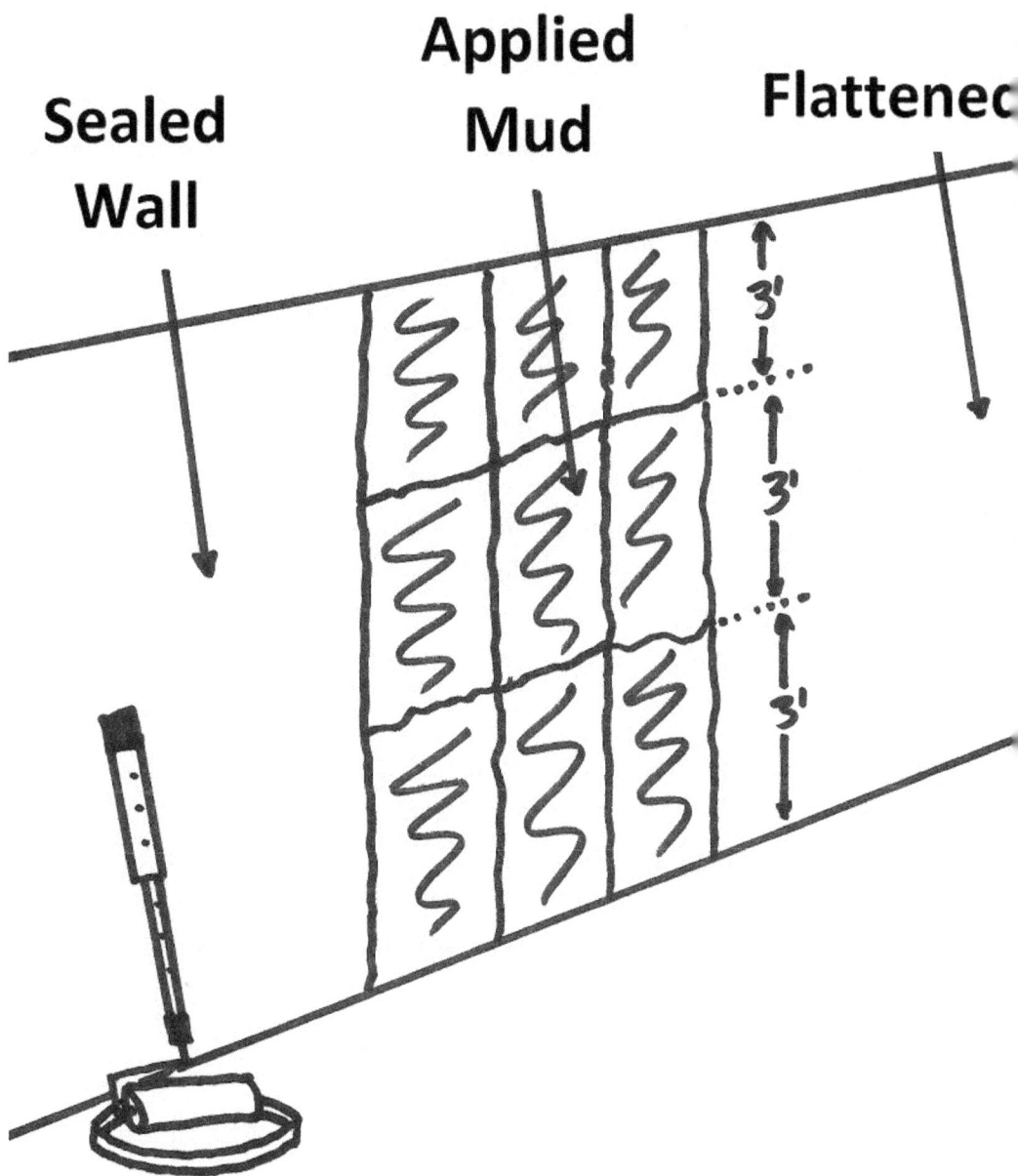

Sealed Wall

Applied Mud

Flattened

3'

3'

3'

Use a broad drywall knife (8" or 10") to flatten out the texture left by the roller. Try not to scrape very much off, just gently pack it down with a laid-down broad knife. It will take some time to develop a light touch and a clean release. That's okay, this gets done again. Leave most of the mud on the wall for this step. Your blade should only have a trace amount if you're packing the mud down instead of scraping it away. Clean your blade on the mud pan after each swipe. When all the textured areas of the wet mud patch have been flattened, scrape some mud from the sides of your bucket to gather material for "picking in the edges." Similar to the patching step described earlier, apply generously to uncoated parts of the wall and sculpt away from inside corners and the edges of obstacles until a thick skin of approximately 2/10" remains.

Move on to another section of wall that directly touches what you just did. The size of the workable section will vary according to your confidence and especially the amount of airflow in the work area. If the drying fans are still running, shut them off now. The skimming process works best in a humid environment.

If the previous section of wall is no longer wet mud but has begun to dry, you may find that as you blend the two sections, the first section's mud pulls away from its place or sticks to your knife. Use more wet mud to fix these minor issues, and try taking a smaller bite of wall on the next section. Try to join the sections wet-to-wet.

Myth #8 – "Topping" compound is for skimming walls

Not true. It's for texturing ceilings.

The type of mud I recommend for skimming walls is **lightweight all-purpose joint compound**. It behaves the best compared to other typed of mud when skimming one section of wall into the previous section. The product sold as "topping" starts drying immediately, and when you try to join to sections of mud that are in different states of dryness, the dry side will stick to the knife and pull away from the wall. Once this happens, you're stuck until everything dries enough to make a new mud repair. This is often the step where young children watching the process learn their first curse words. Use discretion.

When all the wall surfaces have been coated, knock the roller cover back into the mud bucket. Turn on the drying fans if needed and allow the area to dry completely. Nice job!

Chapter 10

Intermediate Sanding

Before applying a second coat of drywall mud, the high spots and ridges left by mud tools need to be scratched away. The most efficient way to physically knock down these lines is to use a professional style pole sander. Unfortunately this method creates the biggest nuisance of this entire process – the dreaded drywall dust of horror. If this doesn't matter, you're in business. Scratch down all the high spots, and don't worry about making it pretty or polishing out voids just yet. You are preparing a flat (ish) surface for the next layer of mud.

A very high end alternative is to use a vacuum equipped power sander to knock down ridges. They are very efficient and mostly dust-free, but mastering the machines is learning arc that probably exceeds the duration of your project. They will be discussed later, but there is a low tech, low cost technique using a shop vacuum and a sanding sponge that collects nearly all the dust before it gets to the floor.

Remove all attachments from the shop vac hose. Hold the hose almost touching the wall, directly below the area you wish to sand, and tilt the hose so that air is forced into the nozzle from above, flowing across the wall from high to low at great speed. The exaggerated picture below shows the optimal angle for maximum dust capture:

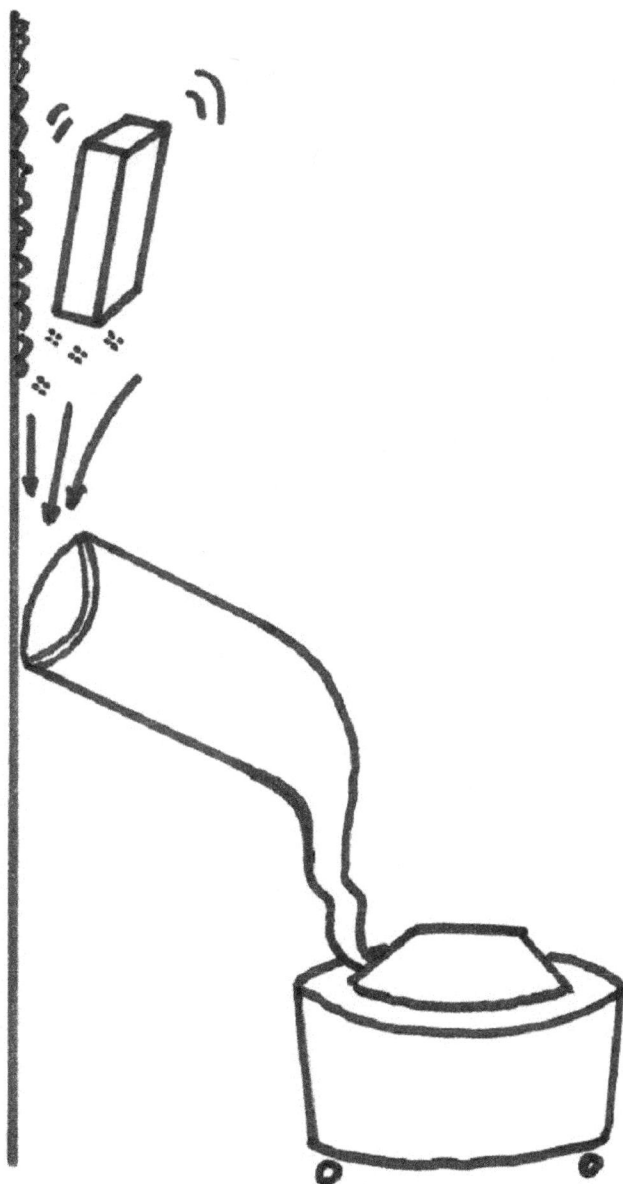

While holding the vacuum hose with one hand, use the other to run the sanding sponge in a circular motion wherever possible. The dust should fall straight into the tube. Take this two-handed operation around the room, knocking down any ridges, lines, high spots and overlap marks left by the mud tools. Don't spend too long on this step or try to make it look nice just yet. There is another coat of mud left to go!

Myth – this shop-vac has a filter, it doesn't need anything else

Picking up drywall dust with a vacuum that's not set up specifically for this fine dust spreads around harmful junk for everyone to breathe. Always use a collection bag paired with a decent filter for this process. All the lungs in the building will thank you.

This intermediate sanding step is not supposed to be a finished product! Don't worry about minor imperfections, or tiny ripples from the drywall paper buried under drywall mud. The second layer of mud will fix them. For now, just dust the walls down so the next layer sticks well.

Chapter 11

Mud Work - Second Skim Coat

Next, the walls get another layer of drywall mud, but instead of leaving most of it behind after applying the mud with either knife or the roller, the bulk of the compound will be scraped back off, leaving a thinner film behind. This fills any voids left by the first coat and dries to a crisp surface that will require a surprisingly little amount of sanding!

The same techniques for knife or roller skimming are used for applying the second layer, except that instead of leaving most of the mud behind, you will be scraping most of it back off after the initial application. The final depth of this second layer should ideally end up about half that of the first layer, by applying generously and removing most of it – leaving about 1/10 of an inch.

You should be able to scrape away most of the mud and leave behind very few traces of tool marks if your intermediate sanding was done thoroughly. The mud will have a tendency to dry out as it is continuously spread, scraped off, and re-used. One option, especially if applying by hand, is to keep a small water bottle handy and stir some directly into the mud pan.

For larger areas on which I use the roller method, I've found it helpful to establish a "source" and a "return" bucket. Roll or scoop from the same bucket, and dump the scrape-off into another. This ensures your skimming mud is fresh and spreadable. When the "return" bucket is full, add some water and remix. It is now the new "source" bucket.

Coat all areas that were done on the first pass, working one wet section of wall into another as you did before. Take the time to butter up the inside corners. Make sure any big repairs underneath have enough mud on them. As this second layer starts to dry it's almost like a glaze forming on your nearly finished product. Just gotta sand, prime, and paint it twice. Sorry.

Chapter 12

Sanding

It's everyone's most hated part of a task like this. The good news is, since you did that second layer of drywall mud, the amount of sanding that's actually needed at this point is manageable with a sanding sponge and a shop vac hose to collect the dust. Refer to the previous diagram showing optimal set-up for this simple operation.

Continue the two-handed operation around the room, checking for and erasing any scratches, ridges, chatter marks and anything not smooth. There should be little dust left on the floor but now would be a great time to sweep it up. Vacuum the top of door frames and the faces of power outlets. Remove any mud that doesn't belong where it is – door and window trim, fire devices, doorknobs and power outlets. The project is ready for the final sanding inspection.

SANDING ALTERNATIVE #1 – ONLY IF A HUGE MESS IS FINE

If you're rehabbing an entire house, or the work area has been contained such that dust is okay, you may save time by using a pole sander followed by a sanding sponge to do the work. The dust falls down, and can be swept up all at once when the sanding is over.

SANDING ALTERNATIVE #2 – THE POWER SANDER

Larger projects may warrant renting or purchasing a vacuum assisted drywall power sander to do the work. The first ones I ever used were made by *Porter Cable*, but I'm not sure if they still make them. *Fes Tool* is another premium brand of sander, but there a lot of manufacturers these days. A search for the generic terms "vacuum+drywall+sander" will yield an impressive variety of results. If you decide to try the power sander, BEWARE they can destroy all your nice mud work if you're not careful! Practice on something that doesn't matter before using it on the walls.

Set up the unit as described by the manufacturer. Choose a sanding disk in the 220 – 120 grit range, and set the rotation speed to the slow side of the range. Place the sanding head on the wall before starting the motor. The vacuum for most of these things can be tool-triggered, but make sure it is running any time the sanding head is spinning.

Constantly move the sanding head in a circular motion around the wall. Avoid long, continuous motions like zig zags or stripes, as these tend to leave ridges in the finished product that only really show up after painting.

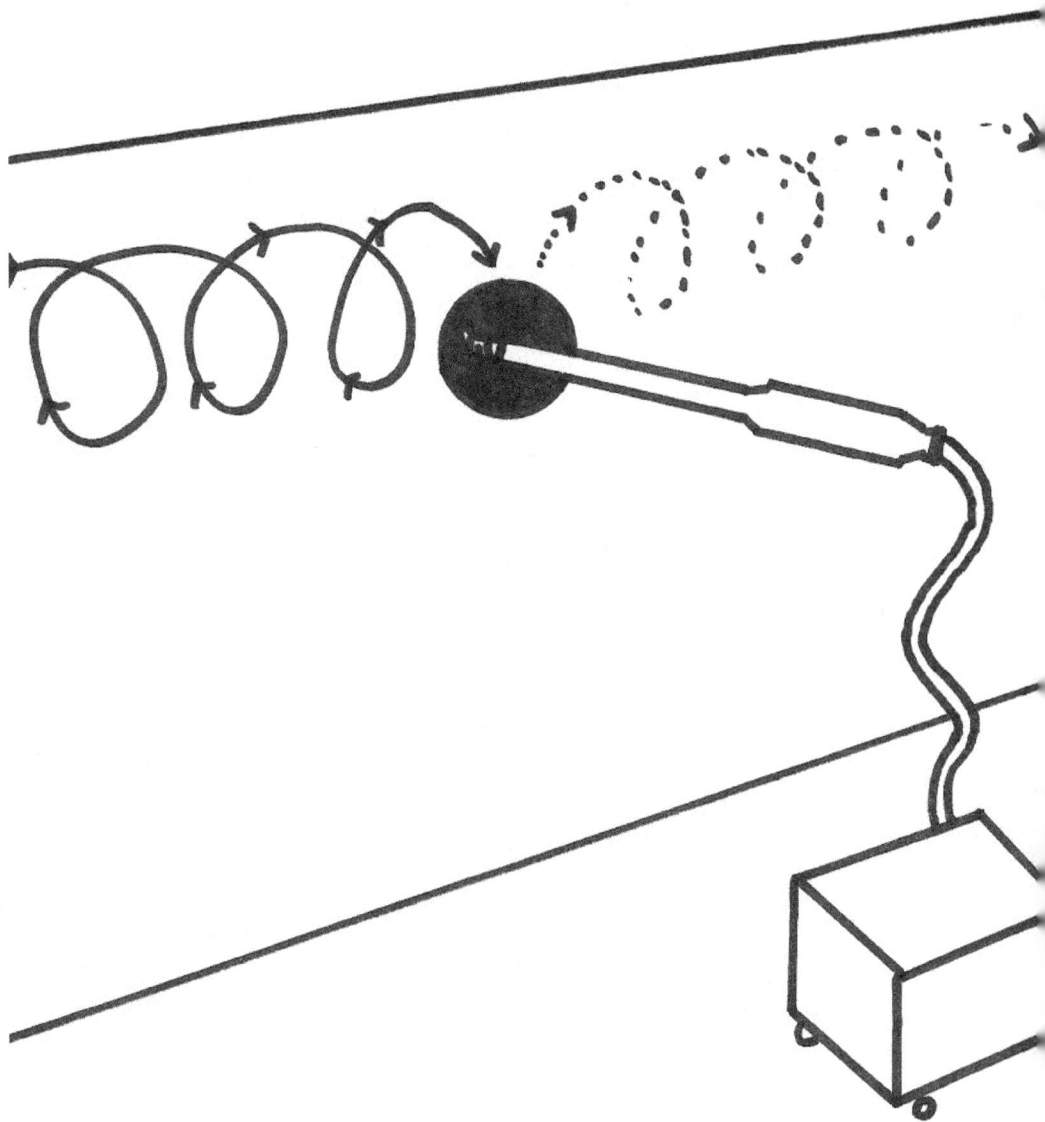

Do not let the spinning sanding head remain in place, for any amount of time, anywhere on the wall! This will dig a deep arc in seconds, and you'll have to make further repairs. Keep it moving constantly, and when you need to stop, power the sanding unit down first, continuing the circular motions until the head stops spinning.

For areas of wall below the waist of the machine operator, it may be helpful for the operator to stand back-to-the-wall, holding the machine with a reverse grip. It is less stress for the lower back to be like this as opposed to pushing forward on an awkward machine all hunched over.

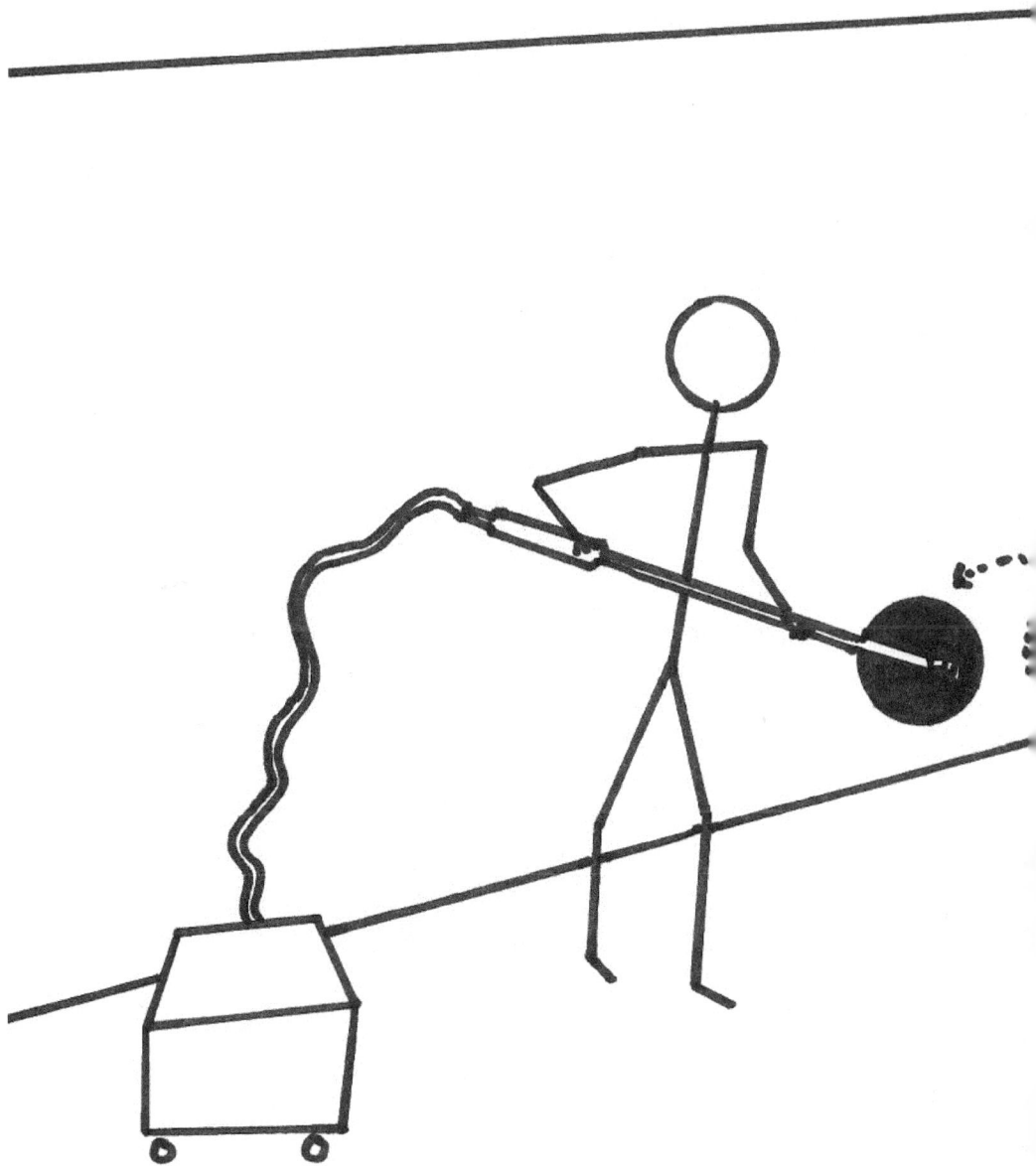

Use the circular motions anywhere the sanding head will fit. If the head gets stuck, don't panic, just kill the power immediately! Those areas the machine can't reach will have to be sanded by hand with a sponge. Be sure to sweep up the dust that does hit the floor. The project is ready for a final sanding inspection.

DROP CEILING MEETS THE WALL

In commercial settings, it is likely the room you are doing has a drop ceiling. I prefer that the interface between wall and ceiling, aka wall molding, has a hairline gap all the way around the room. I use a razor knife or the 4" scraping knife to reinforce this line if there are places where the skimming mud got smushed into the wall mold.

In some cases where the walls are wavy or the ceiling got bent somehow, there may be a sizable gap. These rooms look better with a line of white caulking filling the gap. So once the decision has been made, either caulk the whole room or make a clean line.

Chapter 13

Sanding Inspection

It's amazing what shows up after a coat of primer and paint are applied to the walls. Get a jump start on ironing out flaws by performing a thorough examination of the final sanding job. To do this, you'll need a directional light source, such as a flashlight or portable work lamp. Shine the light *across the wall* to highlight flaws.

To convince yourself of the importance of the direction in which you shine the light, try the simple test of first pointing the light straight into the wall:

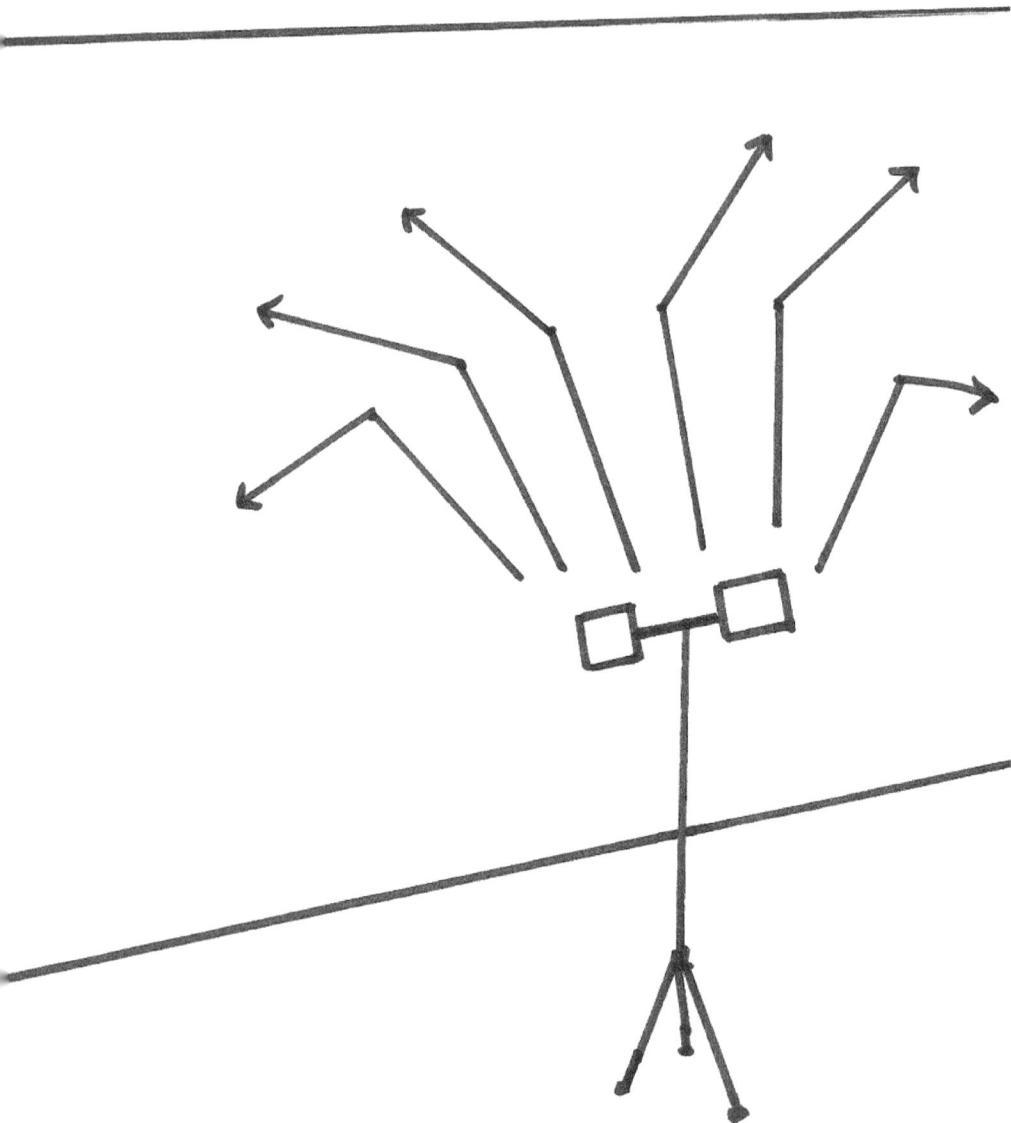

And then with the light shining parallel to the plane of the wall:

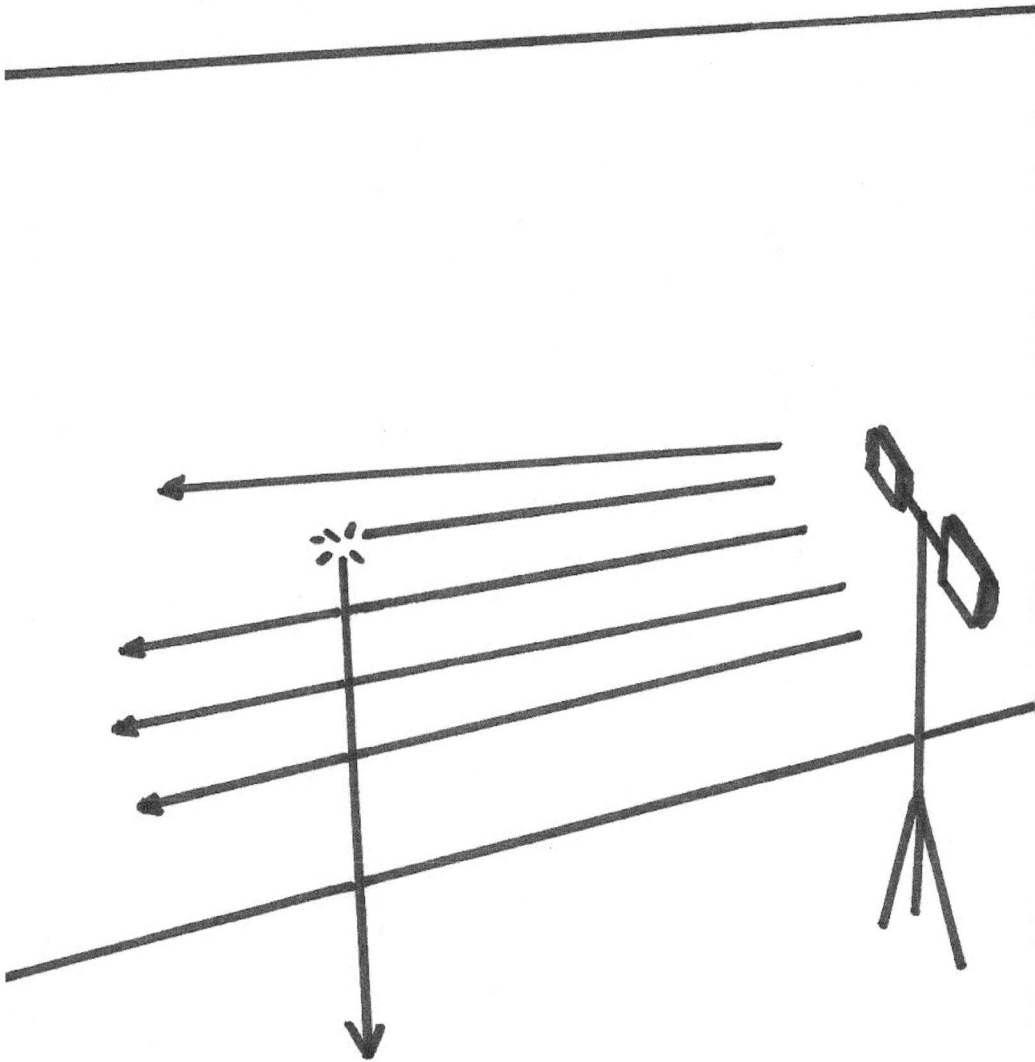

You'll find that the light rays get disturbed by the tiniest flaw, bouncing off it and then into your eye. Natural light, while enhancing the finished room, can interfere with the inspection process by cancelling out light from your work lamp. It's best to pull the shades for this step. Scan the walls from a variety of angles, always keeping the light parallel to the wall, to get the fullest picture of what still needs to be sanded. You may want a helper to shine the light if you are juggling a sanding sponge in one hand and a vacuum hose in the other.

Chapter 14

Final Preparation for Painting

Until now this has been a drywall project. You're now about to switch gears into painting mode. If you have used masking tape to protect trim work during the skimming process, remove it at this time! Get rid of the chunks of mud and potential problems, and lay down fresh masking tape whose only purpose is to catch speckles and drips from the painting process.

Chances are the tape is "hogged up" with mud in certain places, and after the mud gets paint on it, and everything dries, removing masking tape turns into a damaging process. The extra time spent re-taping now will come back to you when fewer repairs are needed down the road.

WHERE TO USE MASKING TAPE

Most weekend painters over-do the masking tape. They lack the confidence in their brush skills to trim around windows, ceiling lines, and cabinets. This is understandable, especially if their only experience has been using bargain basement paint brushes. It's really hard to do a nice job with a cheap paint brush. It's easy to make a mess. Spend the fifteen dollars and get a top shelf, firm, 2.5" – 3" brush and a wire brush for cleaning the bristles when you're done.

With a decent brush in your hands, you only *really* need to apply masking tape to those surfaces that will be speckled by a paint roller. This amounts to any surface that "looks" up – like baseboard tops, backsplash tops, and any trim with a finished (and therefore visible) top edge. Ceiling lines and vertical edges (think cabinets and door casings) turn out better when they are done freehand. Taping every single thing makes more work not just in the time spent applying the tape, but also repairing the damage that *removing* the tape will inevitably cause. Even more, that stuff is expensive!

Chapter 15

Primer Coat

The work area has been sanded, the dust removed, and protections for painting that are appropriate for your situation have been applied. You may have noticed some blistering of drywall paper or previous paint layers underneath the fresh mud. These will be dealt with after the primer dries. For now, everything needs a coat of a decent wall primer.

Just about every paint manufacturer makes a quality wall primer. How much to buy depends on the size of the work area, and those guidelines are printed on the can. They are usually very accurate. Ask the store to add colorant to the primer, at 70% of the full strength formula in whatever color you've chosen for the final look. The tinted primer will help you find flaws, and help to build a solid, monolithic look in the end.

Consider purchasing a strainer bag as all paint products contain solids that can separate on the shelf. The shaking machine at the store gets rid of most of these clumps, but a first class finished product deserves a *two dollar* strainer bag. Get a 5 gallon size to make it easy on yourself.

Straining paint is easy if you're set up properly. Wear some disposable exam gloves. Mount the strainer bag in an empty one gallon can or a clean 5 gallon bucket, and set a one gallon can about half full of water next to the clean bucket. Pour new paint through the bag. When enough paint has gone through, squeeze out the bag directly over the catch vessel:

As the last of the primer or paint is forced through the bag, immediately move the used bag to the water vessel. You can use the grit of the bag and the water of that second vessel to clean the bulk of the paint from your gloves. Now your primer / paint will be free from any chunks or "boogers."

BRUSH WORK – "CUTTING IN"

Pour about a quart of primer into a one gallon can. This will be your "cut pot," or "trim bucket," or whatever else the local painters call it. Use it along with the good quality wall brush to coat areas where the roller can't reach. Where masking tape is used, consider the tape as a guide and a backstop, not really a waterproof barrier. Use a drier brush for trimming against masking tape.

When approaching ceiling lines or vertical trim pieces, load the brush with lots of paint, knock off the excess on one side of your cut pot, then draw a nice wide line about an inch shy of the actual ceiling or trim boundary. Lay up another brush full, and then start working the edge of your drawn line toward the ultimate edge of the surface you are painting:

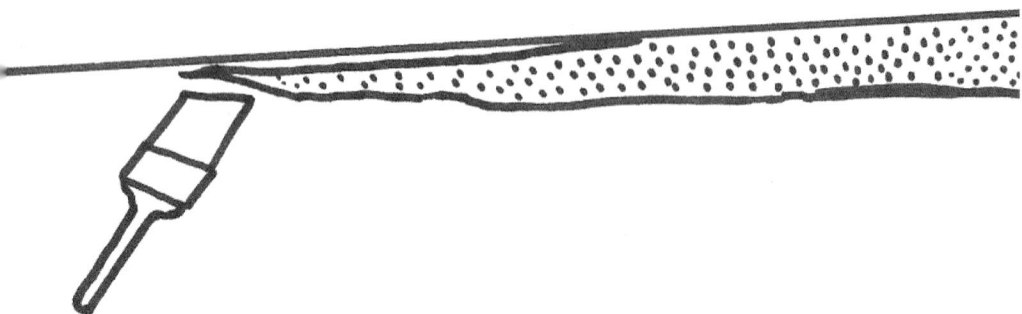

Before you move to the next ladder stop or another on-wall obstacle, be sure you left enough paint on the wall. Get the "cut" as full and streak-free as you can without causing excessive material to drip down the wall.

Myth #9 – Good painters never drip or make mistakes

The old joke goes something like: "How can you tell a good painter from a bad one? … A rag."

It's completely true. A moist cotton rag is the cheapest yet most indispensable tool this project will require. Wipe your fingers *here* instead of on your clothes, and use the rag to keep excess paint off the handle and ferrule of the paint brush. Wrapped around a small drywall knife, a wet rag can help straighten any stray marks left by brush work. Even your drop cloth needs a wiping after catching a drip, so you don't walk into it and then track paint elsewhere.

Apply primer with the brush along all inside corners, door margins, ceiling lines, trim lines, and around power outlets. Trim around sensors, fire alarms, and anywhere the roller needs to get close. Check the open parts of the walls to be sure any drips from brushing have fallen onto the "field."

ROLLING PRIMER

Pour some of the strained primer into a roller tray. The amount depends on the size of roller tray you decide to purchase. It is well worth the extra *three dollars* to buy the bigger tray that holds up to a gallon of liquid. Before touching a new roller sleeve to any paint product, it is **an absolute must** that you take the steps to **de-fuzz the roller sleeve**. All the careful prep work that has been done so far can be cancelled out by a wall that's full of little squiggly coils shed from a new roller sleeve.

They're easy to prevent. Stretch a piece of masking tape from you to any solid object about an arm's length away. Holding the tape in one hand, use the other to run the dry roller over the sticky side, back and forth, until no more lint comes off the sleeve. It's ready to go.

Working out of the roller pan, apply an even coat of primer from floor to ceiling. As a very rough estimate, one full dip from the pan should go floor to ceiling, only the width of the roller. Later coats of finish paint will spread a little farther, but for now the bare mud walls will be amazingly thirsty for this first coat of precious primer. Apply generously.

Roll the walls with a sectional approach. Use natural boundaries like doors, ceilings, and adjacent walls to map out an area of wall that can be rolled in a handful of minutes. The size of the section of wall you can work at any given time will change according to the ambient airflow in the work area. Two sections of wall need to be blended together before the difference in dryness is noticeable. It will matter more when you're applying finish paint, but the priming step is a good time to practice blending wet sections of wall together.

Myth #10 – you gotta draw W's on the walls, like the commercials

People on TV absolutely cannot paint. Making little W's with a paint roller at eye level and expecting the rest to just magically fill in perfectly is downright ridiculous. For each section of wall, apply the paint in vertical stripes, spread it around to an even coat, and then do a final pass of roller without extra paint to lay down the stipple from the application and spreading process.

My favorite commercial in terms of being unrealistic is the guy
who's holding a barely-used brush (actually the cheapest on the

shelf) and he's supposedly painting a small barn blue. The whole thing is painted already, but for some reason he's putting the last dip of paint on the very middle of the barn with a scrappy brush. And loving it. The point is, commercials are not a good reference for painting technique. Put the stuff on, spread it around, and then lay the texture down smooth with a final roller pass. Allow the primer to fully dry before moving to the next steps.

Chapter 16

Fix The Bubbles

Despite all the effort to prevent blisters and bubbles from forming in the first place, and even after layering up two coats of drywall mud, there may be spots of wall that still aren't cooperating. Before proceeding to the painting steps, it's important that these be identified and removed.

You probably noticed these spots in previous phases of the project. While it can be tempting to repair them earlier, I recommend that repairs wait until a primer coat has dried. This way the mud used for the repair can be sanded flush to the plane of the wall. A new mud repair over previously dried mud does not sand well. The two muds are at different hardness and always leave a cleft line or "photograph" effect when sanded.

The best way to check for potential repair spots is to complete an already essential painting step at this stage of the game. The primered walls will *need to be sanded* to achieve a butter-smooth top coat, and the process of sanding the tinted primer can reveal hidden flaws. Using either a drywall sanding sponge or a pole sander, run some sandpaper of 120-220 grit briefly across all surfaces of the wall.

When the trouble spots have been located, use that 4" knife from the stripping process that you've dedicated to being a scraping tool. It should be sharp enough to cut into the edge of a blistered portion. Work the knife around the edge of each blister, feeling for the boundary between loose and stuck. You may be surprised, so let the wall decide where the edges are. After proper scraping, a typical blister field may look something like this:

After scraping away the bad spots, they need to be re-sealed with the same stuff used after stripping the wallcovering. Soak them thoroughly with a brush and allow to dry. In the meantime, there is surely some cleanup that can be done, or you can get a jump start on the brush work of the first finish coat of paint.

When the trouble spots are dry, use either some "regular" drywall mud, "setting type" joint compound commonly called "durabond" or a spackling compound to completely fill the flaws. Allow to dry, then sand them flush to the wall. Finally, apply a coat of primer over the repairs, using the roller wherever possible to achieve a uniform texture effect. "Spot priming" like this with a brush creates a noticeable flat look in a sea of otherwise gentle roller stipple.

Allow the primer to dry completely. Clean out your painting tools to get rid of the solids packed into today's primers. A vigorous rinse under warm (not hot) water, while raking solids away with a wire brush, is enough to patiently clean brushes. For roller sleeves, a stream of warm water and the curved part of a 5-in-1 paint tool is enough to get the job done. Consider purchasing a hand-powered spinner for spin-drying sleeves and brushes. If you want to spend the money, a roller cover cleaner can be had for around $20, and these things are really cool.

Chapter 17

Painting – First Finish Coat

The painting process uses the same motions as the priming process - brush work first, then rolling the walls to a smooth finish. You will notice, perhaps even feel refreshed, that a brush full of paint will go much further over dried primer than the primer did over bare drywall mud. This glide effect will be especially noticeable on the second coat of finish paint.

"Cutting in" ceiling lines need not take years to master, nor do you need to wreck your ceilings with masking tape. Load a high quality brush with paint by dipping and flexing the brush in a shallow can of paint so that the bristles are saturated and the ferrule remains free of material. Knock away excess paint inside the can, and consider only getting paint on one half on the can's interior. Your hands will stay much cleaner throughout the process.

Draw a heavy line horizontally about ½" shy of the actual ceiling. Reload the brush and work the edge of the paint toward the ceiling, making sure to fill the entire corner with wall paint. Here's an edge-on view of a properly "cut" ceiling line:

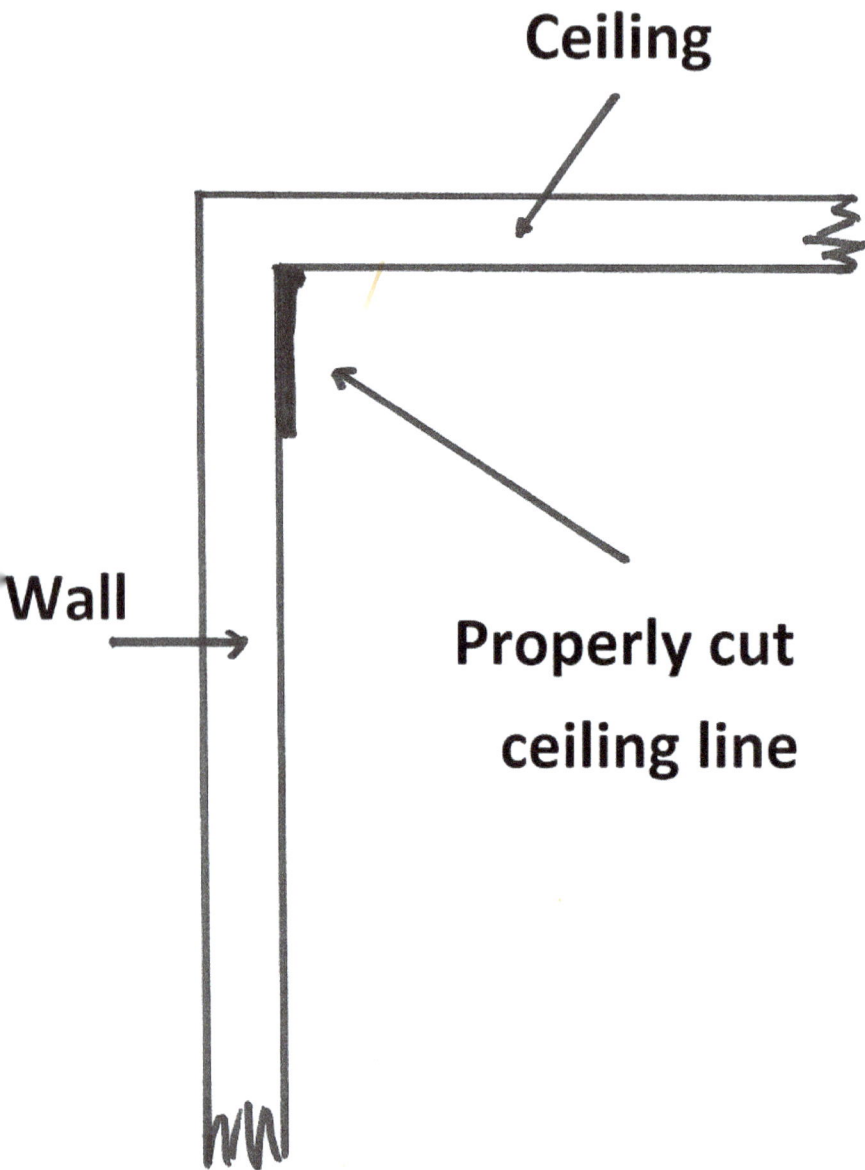

Ceiling

Wall

Properly cut ceiling line

Often when people decide to cut their own lines and forgo the masking tape, they tend to stop short of the actual corner. By using this cautious approach they've actually created a situation of having *three colors* present instead of two. The ceiling is one color, often white. Drywall mud is also white, but may be muted and definitely has no sheen. The walls are their own color. By stopping short of the corner, the third color of "bare mud" is introduced. Walls look much crisper when the entire corner is filled with wall paint.

When all the edges are painted, apply the strained paint with a quality, de-fuzzed roller cover of ½" nap. The material will travel further than the primer did over bare drywall mud. Using a sectional approach, apply the paint, spread it around, and finish each section with a final "dry" pass without reloading more paint.

Careless vertical rolling without attention to pressure can result in heavy lines running vertically or piled up material at the top of the wall. When the paint dries, this heavy edge can create a picture frame effect, showing a noticeable difference between brushed and rolled parts of the wall.

Pay attention to the pressure you use when rolling walls. There will be surprises as the natural terrain of the wall lets you know that no wall is truly flat. Go easy around the edges, and never push down hard to squeeze out more paint. Instead, get another dip. Some painters, especially tall ones, like to use a roller to "echo" the brush line at the ceiling before rolling the field of the wall in vertical stripes. This helps the roller stipple dissolve into the ceiling, and gives an easy target for where to stop the up-stroke and head back down when completing the final passes on a section of wall.

Cut line from brush

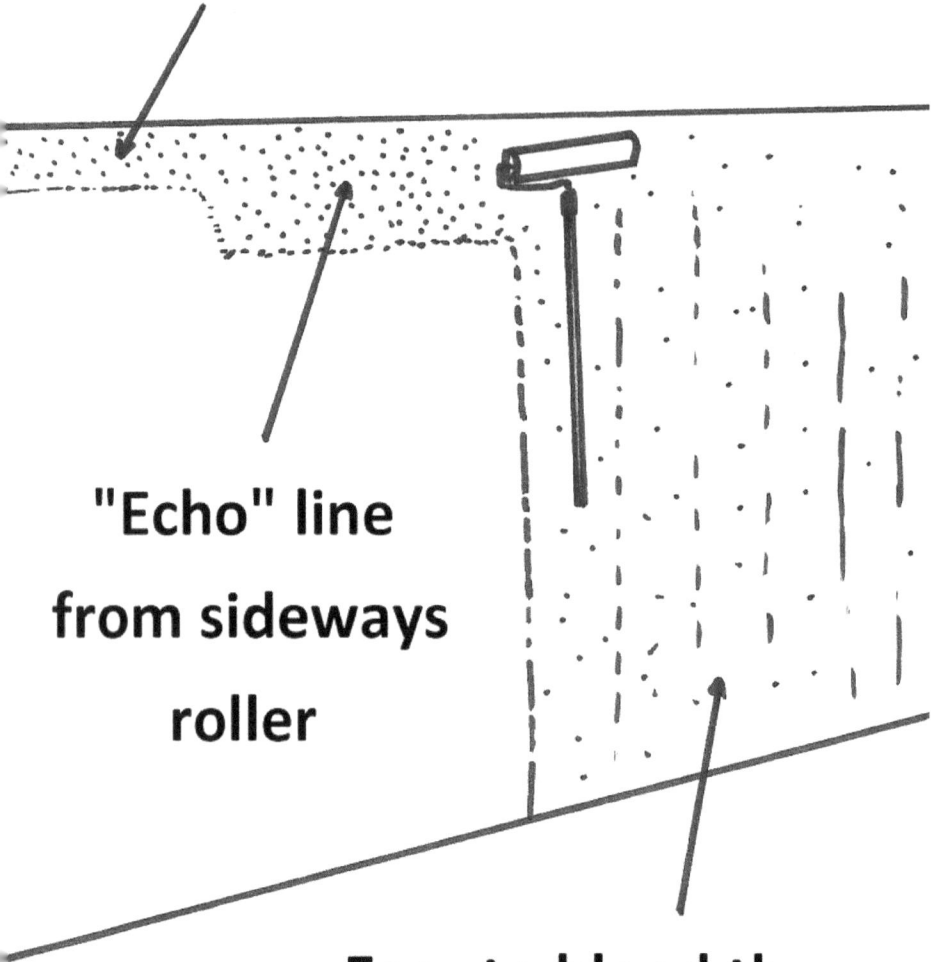

"Echo" line from sideways roller

Easy to blend the rolled wall with cut-in

Finally, allow the area to dry completely, preferably overnight, before proceeding to the next step.

Chapter 18

Painting – Second Finish Coat

You have one last opportunity to fix any remaining flaws. There should not be many at this point if the steps laid out in this course have been fully realized. A quick sanding of the painted walls doesn't hurt anything and gives your eyes one last lap around the project. Fix any dings with spackling, sand when dry and spot "prime" as before **using the finish paint** as primer in this case.

Brush strokes can be longer as the glide factor is about double on this second coat. Roller dips will go further than the previous coat, and maybe two to three times further than the primer did. This is a great time to consider an advanced painting concept - the pattern of roller strokes as you move through an area.

It's easy and natural to use the "big V" pattern as you move down the wall, but it won't result in the best possible look when everything dries.

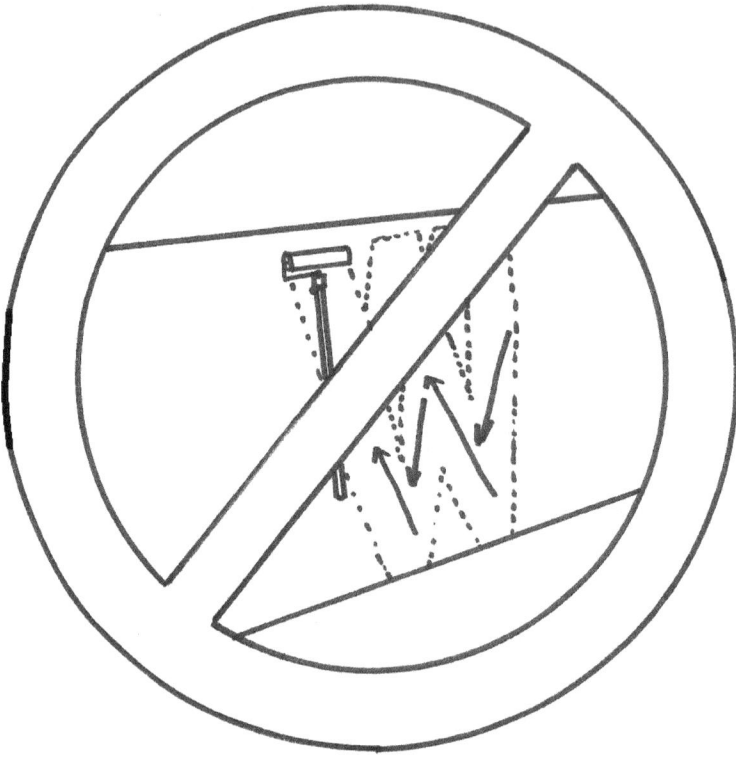

The reason for this is the roller stipple is pointing upwards after an up-stroke, and pointing down after a down-stroke. It dries in somewhat the same shape as it's applied. By making giant isosceles triangles with your finishing strokes, the cured paint looks strange and striped under certain lighting conditions.

Try to leave all the roller stipple facing downward. Less light will reflect toward peoples' eyes and the painted wall seems to lose its boundaries, becoming more like a pillow of color.

For each section of wall, apply the paint and spread it around as discussed above. Pay careful attention to the final moves as you smooth out what you've applied. Final strokes should be ceiling-to-floor, down stroke last. Move the roller to the next vertical stripe on the up stroke, completing the entire shift before the roller gets approximately thigh-high. The final finish stroke will be downward, erasing the angled approach from the previous stripe.

Shown below is a long wall in the process of being rolled. The roller is currently at the top of an up-stroke during the final swipes of the process. Note the all previous swipes finish on the down stroke. The little arrows denote the direction of the stipple.

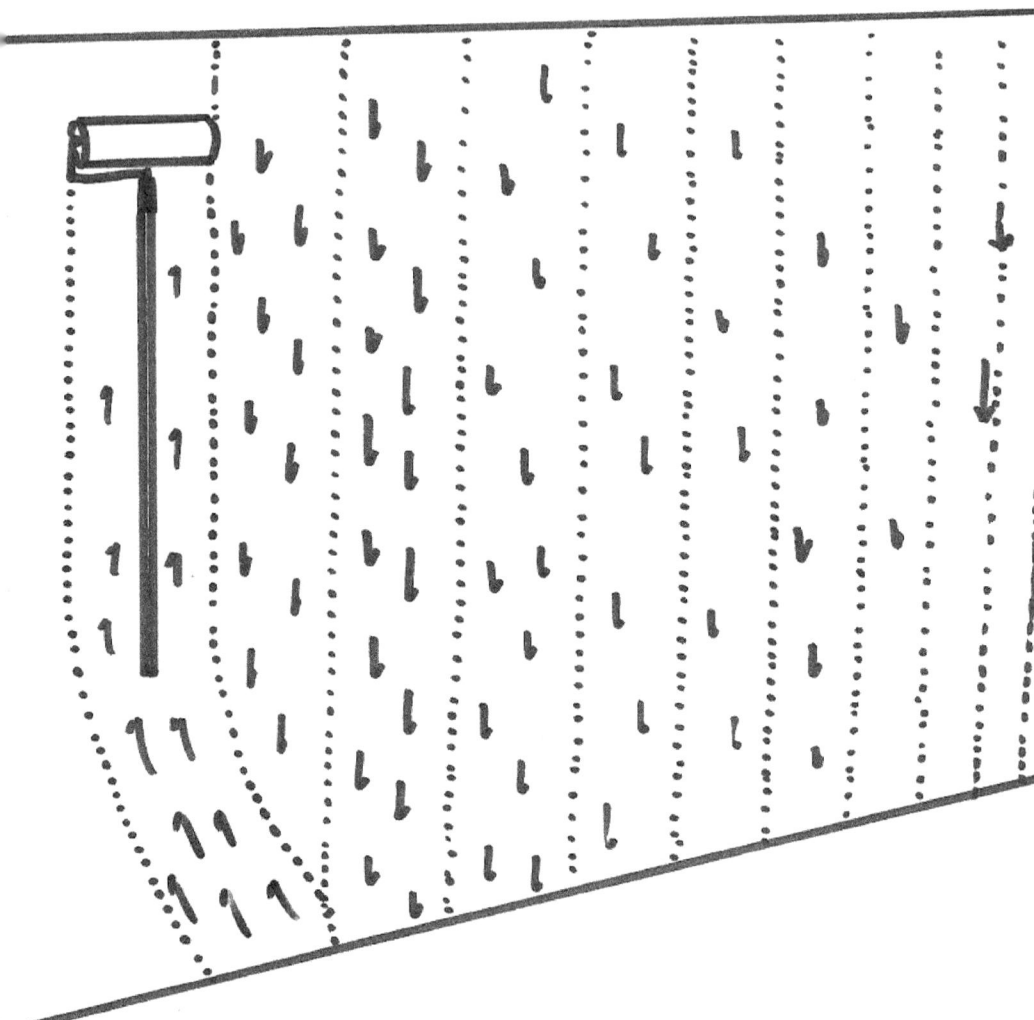

REVOMAL OF MASKING TAPE

The debate continues every day about when is the best time to remove tape. Careful removal soon after painting takes advantage of the soft uncured paint, but risks peeling away what needs to stay. Waiting a day is probably best, but in most cases I cannot wait any longer than a few minutes.

To remove masking tape soon after painting, run a new, clean utility knife along any edges that may cause lifting of wall paint. You don't have to dig hard, just score the surface. Peel it away in such a manner as to minimize damage to the substrate. Often this means a perpendicular pull, but not always. Take your time and adjust your technique as necessary.

PUT THE ROOM TOGETHER

After the paint dries it's time to replace all the switch plates and outlet covers. It was worth the extra minutes to replace the screws at the time the plates are removed, because now you don't have to look for them. Thermostats can go back on, but let the paint fully cure before installing paintings or other items that will remain in contact with the wall surface.

CONGRATULATIONS!

You've taken the steps to achieve the best possible appearance for your interior refresh. The new surface will be durable for years and easy to repair when things do happen, especially with your new skills gained from this experience. Enjoy the new space!

www.ingramcontent.com/pod-product-compliance
Lightning Source LLC
Chambersburg PA
CBHW070819050426

42452CB00011B/2110